Cookbook

The Best of Dinner & a Movie's Delectable Dishes

Recipes by Claud Mann

Written by Kimberlee Carlson, Heather Johnson & Claud Mann

With Illustrations by Robert Clyde Anderson

Andrews McMeel
Publishing

Kansas City

Printed in Canada.

Library of Congress Cataloging-in-Publication Data

Mann, Claud.
      Dinner & a movie cookbook : recipes / by Claud Mann : with
illustrations by Robert Clyde Anderson : written by Kimberlee
Carlson, Heather Johnson & Claud Mann. — 1st ed.
             p.   cm.
      ISBN 0-7407-0321-8 (pbk.)
      1. Cookery. 2. Dinner & a movie (Television program)
I. Carlson, Kimberlee. II. Title. III. Title: Dinner and a movie cookbook.
TX714.M339   1999
641.5—dc21

99-37548
CIP

Produced by Lionheart Books, Ltd.
Atlanta, Georgia 30341

Published by Andrews McMeel Publishing,
an Andrews McMeel Universal Company
4520 Main Street
Kansas City, Missouri 64111

www.andrewsmcmeel.com

Table of Contents

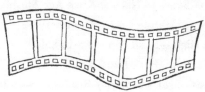

Chef's Introduction 8

9 to 5—Male Chauvinist Pig 10

Airplane—Thai Noodles with Airplane Nuts 12

Arachnophobia —Creepy Crawly Crab Legs 14

Baby Boom —Offspring Rolls (or "Little Bundles of Joy") 16

Back to the Future—Travelin' Through Thyme and Onion Tart 18

Beetlejuice —Dearly Departed Sole 20

Bill & Ted's Excellent Adventure—Napoleon "Bone-Apart" Snapper Sandwiches . . 22

The Blue Lagoon—Young-and-Naked Fish Kabobs with Mango Tiki Sauce 24

Blue Steel—High Caliber Shells 26

The Blues Brothers—Funky Chicken 28

The Breakfast Club—Breakfast Club Sandwich 30

Brewster's Millions —"Rolling in Dough" Homemade Ballpark Pretzels 32

The 'burbs—Classic Cul-de-Sac Mac 'N Cheese 34

Carrie—Carrie's Prom Crisp 36

A Christmas Carol—Scrooge's Turkey Legs with Crispy Gruel Stuffing 38

A Christmas Story—Edible Fruitcake ... No, Really! 40

Coal Miner's Daughter—Butcher Holler Ham Hocks and Collards 42

The Cutting Edge—Triple Axel Rotisserie Chicken 44

D.O.A.—Biscuits to Die For (with One Foot in the Gravy) 46

Date with an Angel—Heavenly Wings 48

Deceived—Super Extra Meaty Meatloaf 50

Diamonds Are Forever—Bon Bons ... James Bon Bons 52

Dirty Dancing—Bumpin' Grinders (with Smoldering Loins) 54

Don't Tell Mom the Babysitter's Dead—Christina Applecake 56

Dracula: Dead and Loving It—Nosferatuna Melts 58

Dragnet—Just the Facts, Ham 60

Dumb and Dumber—Soup on a Stick 62

Encino Man—Missing Link Sausage Nachos & Ice Age Slushies 64

Fame—I Want Liver Forever, I Wanna Learn How to Fry! .66

Fast Times at Ridgemont High—Sean Penne Pasta Salad .68

Flashdance—Jennifer's Steamin' Pork Buns 70

The Flintstones' Christmas Carol—Standing Rib Roast with Rockshire Pudding . . .72

Footloose—Kevin Bacon and Cheese Hush Puppies 74

The Golden Child—The Chosen Won Ton Soup 76

Goldfinger—Golden Ladyfingers 78

Grumpy Old Men—Young at Hearts of Romaine Seizure Salad 80

Harry and the Hendersons—Bigfoot Longs 82

Honey, I Shrunk the Kids—Shrunken Shanks with Pygmy Veggies in Red Wine
  Reduction 84

Hook—Peter Pancakes with Lost Boysenberry Syrup 86

Jaws—Man Eating Shark ... and Loving It 88

The Jerk—Big Jerked Chicken 90

L.A. Story—New Age Baloney 92

Look Who's Talking Too—Bite Your Tongue Tacos 94

Medicine Man—Miraculously Cured Salmon (with a Rapidly Disappearing Rain Forest
  Salad) 96

The Money Pit—Fall Apart Pot Roast 98

Moving—This Side-Upside-Down Cake 100

Mr. Nanny—Hollywood (Hulk) Hoagies 102

My Girl 2—Girls Just Wanna Have Flan 104

My Stepmother Is an Alien—Extraterrestrial Tempura 106

National Lampoon's Animal House—Bluto's Beer Chili 108

National Lampoon's Vacation—Road Trip Tri-Tip 110

An Officer and a Gentleman—Sergeant Foley's Drop and Give Me 20-Bean Salad
  (topped with Moody and Misunderstood Zack Mayo) 112

Only the Lonely—Irish Stew for One 114

The Outsiders—"Pony Boy" Fries and "Cherry Valence" Pie 116

Point of No Return—Bridget Fondue 118

Pretty Woman—Julia's Angel Hair Puttanesca 120

Raiders of the Lost Ark—Extra Cheesy Spielburgers 122

Real Men—Real Men's Quiche 124

Risky Business—Tommy's Tighty Whitey Whitefish
  (with Oh So Satisfying Sauce Mornay) 126

Roadhouse—Swayze's Cracked Ribs and Black-eyed Peas 128

Saturday Night Fever—Tony Manero's Mozzarella Marinara 130

Sleeping with the Enemy—Pecan Someone Your Own Size Pie 132

Smokey and the Bandit—Breaker. . .Breaker Banana Cream Pie 134

Spaceballs—May the Borscht Be with You 136

Stayin' Alive —Italian Scallion Risotto 138

Stripes—Be All That You Can Beef Stroganoff 140

Thelma & Louise—Two Hot Peppers on the Lamb 142

Tootsie—What's Under Your Skirt Steak? 144

Trading Places—Celery (Root of All Evil) Soup with Pork Belly Croutons 146

Twins—Mussels and Shrimp 148

Urban Cowboy—"No Bull" Tequila Fajitas 150

A View to a Kill—Ice-Cold War Martinis and Secret Spy Snacks 152

War Games—Nuclear Subs with Dressing of the Former Soviet Union 154

War of the Roses—Mouthwatering Kathleen Turnovers 156

What About Bob?—Baby Steppin' Kabobs 158

Know Your Terms! (Glossary) 160

Weights and Measurements 164

Bare Bones Essential Equipment 168

Goods to Keep on Hand 169

More Annoying Tips from Claud Mann, the TBS Food Guy 170

Index 172

Acknowledgments 176

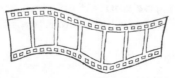

Chef's Introduction

Five years ago the nice people at TBS (and they really are nice) asked me to come up with recipes for various titles in their movie library. Instantly intrigued, I said, "I don't understand."

Then they explained the concept for the show. Every Friday night a captivating and charismatic couple would cook up a meal inspired by that night's mesmerizing movie. I said, "By George! Where do I sign up?"

Sharpening my pencil, my chef's knife and my wits, I retired to the state-of-the-art TBS test kitchen and the rest is history . . . or maybe histrionics, depending on your favorite episode.

The following recipes are some of our favorites. Just remember that a recipe is nothing more than a road map. If you want to take a few side trips or head off in an entirely different direction, go right ahead. I just hope that you have as much fun making them as we did.

And now, although no one asked, I would like to leave you with:

Claud's 10 Kitchen Commandments®

1. **Keep your knives sharp. As a matter of fact, if all you have are cheap, dull knives, don't read any further until you've thrown them out and bought just one good one.**

2. **Roll up your sleeves and use your hands whenever possible.**

3. **Never clean up if you can help it . . . hey, you did the cooking.**

4. **Make it a point to physically remove anyone from the kitchen that makes scornful remarks or backhanded inquiries about the fat, sugar, cholesterol or caloric content of any meal that you are preparing.**

5. **Always give yourself an extra hour. (When you're relaxed, you can have more fun.)**

6. Constantly taste, taste, taste!

7. Get your sauté pans nice and hot and don't worry about a little smoke.

8. Discard bottled herbs and spices if purchased during a previous presidential administration. Smell them—they should have a discernable aroma. If not, might I suggest substituting pencil shavings, which are significantly cheaper and taste just about the same.

9. Whenever a guest offers to bring "a bottle of something," ask for a gallon of extra-virgin olive oil.

10. Always try to cook enough to offer a meal to a neighbor that lives alone. If you don't know them, it's a fine way to get started. (Plus, if more of us bothered to feed each other, the world would be a nicer place.)

Cheers,
Claud Mann
(The TBS Food Guy)

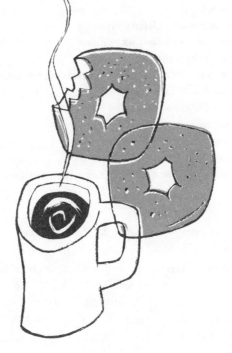

Male Chauvinist Pig

9 to 5
(1980)

This glass-ceiling favorite is popular with pork lovers everywhere, regardless of gender.

For the Pork Roast:
1 2–3 lb boneless center loin pork roast
1/4 tsp ground bay leaf
1/2 tsp ground clove
1/2 tsp ground cinnamon
2 tsp freshly ground black pepper
2 tsp kosher salt
1 Tbsp fresh rosemary, finely chopped
8 cloves garlic, cut into slivers

For the Cabbage:
2 Tbsp butter
1 yellow onion, thinly sliced
6 cups red cabbage, shredded
3 Tbsp cider vinegar
3 Tbsp honey (feel free to substitute Skinny & Sweet)
1/2 cup dark beer
1/2 cup chicken stock
1/4 tsp celery seed
Salt and pepper to taste
4 Tbsp Italian parsley, chopped
1 bottle window cleaner (for glass ceiling)

Chew on This

Because contemporary pork is no longer bred for lard, it's much more healthful than its plump predecessor. One ounce of lean pork contains about 2 grams of fat—as compared to 16 grams for the same amount of peanut butter. So next time you're hungry for a snack, try a pork–and–jelly sandwich.

1. Adjust oven rack position to the upper middle of the oven and preheat to 475°F.

2. Tie 'Em Up: Cut a length of twine about 6 times the length of the rascal you're about to lasso. Make a slip knot and drop it over the end that's not kicking. Continue by making a series of half hitches until you've used up your slack. (By this time he may have stopped struggling and will listen to reason . . . Nah.)

3. Rub It In: In a small bowl, combine the bay leaf, clove, cinnamon, pepper, salt and rosemary. Rub spice mixture into meat. If your chauvinist gets suspicious, tell him it's a new blend of Old Spice.

4. Stud the Stud with Garlic: Pierce the pork in 15-20 spots with a paring knife or skewer and insert the garlic slivers into each opening.

5. Roast 'Em Up: Place the roast on a rack in a roasting pan. Slide the pan into the oven for 30 minutes. After 30 minutes, remove the roast from the oven and reduce the oven temperature to 325°F. Allow the oven to cool before returning the meat to the oven (about 20 minutes). Cook for a final 20-30 minutes, to an internal temperature of 150°F. Let rest for 15 minutes before carving into slices.

6. Make the Bed: Melt the butter in a medium saucepan over medium heat. Add the onions and sauté until limp, about 3 minutes. Add the remaining ingredients, cover, and cook for 15-20 minutes. Toss with chopped parsley just before serving. Arrange slices of roast over bed of cabbage.

7. Savor the Moment: Now you've got your male chauvinist pig just the way you want him: tasteful, submissive, and served on a bed of your own choosing (in this case, cabbage).

Yield: 6 servings

Food for Thought

Most popular politically incorrect food names:
honeybun, sugarpie, peaches, peanut, pumpkin, bundt cake, head cheese, pork butt, java drawers.

Thai Noodles with Airplane Nuts

Airplane
(1980)

When we think flying, we think nuts. This high-flying recipe uses plenty of 'em, and with the cost of airline tickets, these crunchy, in-flight treats don't come cheap. So next time you fly, hold onto your nuts. And don't call us Shirley.

For the Noodles:
2 chicken breasts, skinned and boned
2 Tbsp dry sherry
3 Tbsp soy sauce
1/4 cup peanut oil
5 cloves garlic, peeled and finely chopped
1 serrano or jalapeño pepper, peeled and finely chopped
1 Tbsp shredded pickled ginger
2 eggs, beaten
1 cup (or 8 flight-sized bags) plain peanuts, coarsely chopped
1/2 yellow bell pepper, sliced into 1/2-inch strips
1 cup mung bean sprouts
1/2 lb spaghetti or vermicelli
1 Tbsp sugar
2 Tbsp fish sauce (if unavailable, use anchovy paste)
1 Tbsp ketchup
3 scallions, cut into 1-inch lengths

For the Garnish:
3 limes, cut into quarters
1 tsp red pepper flakes
1/4 cup peanuts, crushed
1/4 cup mint leaves, coarsely chopped
1/4 cup cilantro leaves
1 air-sickness bag (for leftovers)

1. Slice the chicken into thin strips and place in a small bowl. Add the sherry and half of the soy sauce. Cover, set aside, and remember, everyone is counting on you.

2. Cook the pasta *al dente*. Rinse well with cold water, drain, and set aside.

INSIDE SCOOP

Peanut oil is the oil most often used by Chinese chefs for wok cooking because it can be heated to well over 400 °F before it smokes or burns.

3. Prepare all ingredients and place where they can be quickly reached during the stir fry. Avoid touching eyes and sensitive areas of self and others after cutting chili peppers.

4. Using a wok or large cast-iron skillet, heat the peanut oil on high heat. Add the garlic, serrano pepper, and pickled ginger and stir fry until light brown and fragrant.

5. Drain excess marinade from chicken and add to the wok along with the beaten eggs. Stir fry for 2 minutes and remember, everyone is counting on you.

6. Run cold water on any blistered areas of face or hands from oil splatters in steps 4 and 5.

7. Add the bell pepper, pasta, and half of the bean sprouts. Stir fry for another minute, and remember, everyone is counting on you.

8. Add the remaining soy sauce, peanuts, ketchup, fish sauce, and sugar. Cook for another minute, stirring often.

9. Mix in the scallions and transfer to a serving platter. Garnish with the remaining bean sprouts, fresh mint, cilantro, lime quarters, red pepper flakes, and peanuts.

10. At this point your guests may begin to smell something wonderful coming from the kitchen, and wonder what it is. (A large room with pots, pans, and a stove, but that's not important right now.)
Yield: 4 servings

ARE WE GOIN' NUTS?

In 1998 the Department of Transportation ordered the airline industry to supply goober-free seating areas for any passengers with peanut allergies. (Does this mean no "Andy Griffith" reruns?)

Chew on This

Before the Farrelly Brothers, the Hudlin Brothers or the Coen Brothers hit the filmmaking scene, the Zucker Brothers (along with their friend Jim Abrahams) had already proven that brotherly bonds could produce big box office. *Airplane* set the standard for a string of successful Zucker/Abrahams film parodies, including *Naked Gun* and *Hot Shots*.

DID YOU KNOW?

Actor James Arness (Marshall Matt Dillon of TV's "Gunsmoke") and Peter Graves (Captain Oveur) are brothers.

Creepy Crawly Crab Legs

Arachnophobia
(1990)

We couldn't see wolfing down spider legs dipped in butter (can you imagine our test kitchen crawling with spiders?) so we chose a fellow member of the phylum Arthropoda—crabs. Proof that you can't judge a crustacean by its cover, these crab legs may look creepy but their delicious taste will leave you screaming with delight.

For the Curry Sauce:
2 medium tomatoes
2 Tbsp olive oil
1 tsp fresh ginger, grated
1 Tbsp mild curry powder
1/2 cup dry sherry

For the Lemon-Butter:
1/2 stick butter (4 oz)
2 Tbsp parsley, finely chopped
2 Tbsp onion, grated
1-2 tsp hot pepper sauce
2 Tbsp fresh lemon juice

For the Crab Legs:
6-8 frozen king crab legs, defrosted
**The number of a good exterminator (or a copy of
 Charlotte's Web)**

1. Search kitchen cupboards, cracks, and corners for any lurking, malevolent presence waiting to suck the life out of you, your loved ones, or dining companions. If you survive, proceed to step 2.

2. **Make the Curry Sauce:** Peel, seed, and finely chop the tomatoes. Heat the olive oil in a small saucepan over medium heat. Add the ginger and curry powder and sauté until fragrant, about 45 seconds. Add the tomatoes and sherry and simmer 20 minutes or until thickened. Season to taste with salt & pepper.

3. **Make the Lemon-Butter:** Combine the butter, parsley, onion, pepper sauce, and lemon juice in a small saucepan over low heat. Cook until melted; keep warm until use.

Chew on This

Although a significant percentage of the world's population happily includes insects as an important part of their diet we recommend spiders not be substituted for crab. Crickets, on the other hand, might not be bad at all.

4. Prepare the crab legs: Split the shells lengthwise and cut into manageable pieces. Brush each piece with your choice of sauce.

5. Place the crab legs cut-side up on a broiler pan and broil until lightly browned and heated through, about 4 minutes.

6. Serve with plenty of extra sauce and a semi-dry, anti-venom serum of a good vintage.

7. Spin a Web of Deceit All Your Own: Tell your guests a spider-sighting left you too scared to leave your seat so obviously someone else will have to do the dishes.

Yield: 4 servings

Food for Thought

Industry insiders tell us there's an *Arachnophobia* sequel in the works called *Alloxaphobia* (the fear of opinions). It features a 50–foot–tall, hot–air–filled William F. Buckley descending upon an unsuspecting small town.

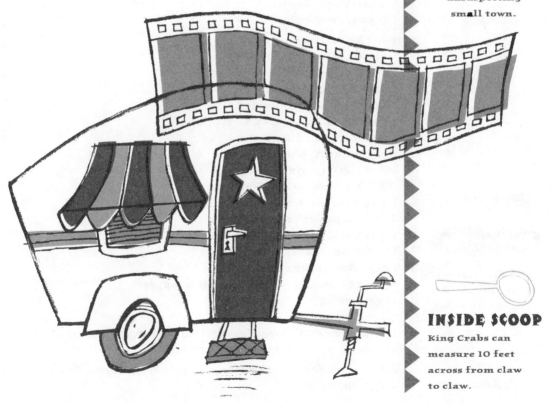

INSIDE SCOOP

King Crabs can measure 10 feet across from claw to claw.

Offspring Rolls (or "Little Bundles of Joy")

Baby Boom
(1987)

Like children, our offspring rolls require a little tender loving care—but with the proper nurturing, they'll grow up to be the kind of party food that'll make you proud.

For the Seasoning:
3 Tbsp sugar
1 Tbsp salt
1/4 tsp chili paste
1/2 cup coconut milk
1/4 cup soy sauce
1/3 cup rice vinegar
1 Tbsp corn starch

For the Filling:
5 dried Chinese mushrooms
1 2-oz package Chinese rice sticks
Peanut oil, as needed
1 Tbsp ginger root, grated
1 Tbsp garlic, peeled and chopped
1 serrano chili, finely diced
1 cup peanuts, crushed
1/2 cup celery, finely diced
1/2 cup yellow onion, finely diced
1/2 cup carrot, finely diced
2 cups napa cabbage, shredded
1/4 cup scallions, thinly sliced
1/2 cup water chestnuts, minced
1 cup cilantro, chopped
1 package won ton or spring roll wrappers
1 egg, beaten

1. Make the Filling: Combine and whisk together the seasoning ingredients in a small mixing bowl. Set aside.

2. Place the dried mushrooms and rice sticks in separate bowls and cover with boiling water.

Chew on This

A smaller version of the egg roll, the spring roll is the traditional food of the Chinese New Year which, coincidentally, occurs in the spring.

3. Allow the mushrooms to soak 15-20 minutes; drain, slice as thinly as possible and set aside. Drain the rice noodles and set aside.

4. Place a wok or large cast-iron skillet over medium heat and add 3 tablespoons of peanut oil. Add the ginger, garlic, serrano pepper and peanuts and slowly stir fry for about a minute.

5. Add the celery, onion and carrot and continue stir frying until they soften, about 2 minutes.

6. Mix in the napa cabbage, scallions, water chestnuts and sliced mushrooms. Continue cooking 3 to 4 minutes before raising the heat to high, whisking together the seasoning mixture and adding it all at once to the center of the pan. Cook and stir until the mixture thickens, about 3 minutes.

7. Spread out the hot mixture on a cookie sheet and allow to cool completely. Mix in the rice noodles and cilantro; taste and adjust seasonings as desired.

8. Make the Offspring Rolls: Shape 2 tablespoons of filling into a small cylinder and place it diagonally across the wrapper. Fold the point of the wrapper closest to you over the filling, tucking in the end. Brush the top corner with a little egg before folding in the sides and roll up as tightly as possible.

9. Heat 2 inches of peanut oil in a heavy skillet over medium-high heat until one end of a roll dipped in the oil sizzles rapidly on contact.

10. Cook the offspring rolls in batches of five or six until golden, about 4 minutes. Turn once halfway through cooking.

11. Serve hot with Hoisin sauce, Chinese mustard or anything else that sounds tasty.
Yield: 20 rolls

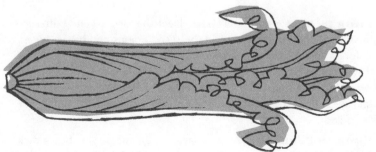

INSIDE SCOOP

When American soldiers returned home from World War II, the U.S. experienced an explosion of births, or a "baby boom." Sociologists define "baby boomers" as those Americans born from 1946 to 1964. Approximately 76 million Americans were born during this 18-year period. In 1999, boomers are between 35 and 53 years old, and represent about 29 percent of the U.S. population.

Travelin' Through Thyme and Onion Tart

Back to the Future

(1985)

Traveling through time is a breeze if a few simple rules are followed:
1. Always reset your watch.
2. Never date your mom.
3. Never do anything that would cause you not to be born (see #2).
4. Never leave potato salad in a hot car.

For the Thyme and Onion Filling:
1 medium white onion, thinly diced
2 medium red onions, thinly sliced
2 Tbsp extra-virgin olive oil
1 tsp light brown sugar
1 Tbsp fresh thyme, chopped
1/2 cup light-bodied red wine, Beaujolais is nice
Salt and freshly ground black pepper

For the Tart Shell and Toppings:
1 sheet frozen puff pastry dough (the most popular national
   brand contains 2 10-inch sheets)
1 egg beaten with 1 Tbsp cold water
1/2 cup grated Parmesan cheese
15 tasty black olives, pitted and chopped
1 6-oz jar artichoke hearts in water, drained and quartered
A little thyme on your hands

1. Time to Make the Filling: Heat the olive oil and butter in a large skillet over medium heat. Add the sliced onions and brown sugar; cook for 15 minutes, stirring often. Add the red wine and increase the heat to medium high. Continue cooking about 10 minutes, until the wine is completely evaporated and the onions have the consistency of thick marmalade. Stir in the thyme, season to taste with salt and pepper. Set aside to cool.

2. Time to Form the Tart: Place a large cookie sheet on a rack in the lower third of the oven and preheat to 425°F. Lay out the puff

Chew on This

When cutting onions, tearing is caused by 2 enzymes that, when combined, create that all-too-familiar eye irritation. Some tricks to lessen the effect include:

1 Use the sharpest knife possible.

2 Refrigerate the onions before cutting.

3 Cut directly under the range-top exhaust vent.

pastry sheet flat on a lightly floured surface. Gently roll the dough to a 10-inch square, dusting with a little flour to avoid sticking. Transfer the dough to a well-buttered sheet of aluminum foil.

3. Using a small pastry brush, paint a 1-inch border of the egg mixture around the perimeter of the pastry square. One at a time, fold over each eggwashed edge to create an inch-wide double thickness border around the tart; brush the egg mixture over the doubled edge. In the area inside the border, use the tines of a fork to lightly prick the dough at 1/2-inch intervals. This will prevent the bottom crust from puffing.

4. Time to Fill: Sprinkle 1/4 cup of the Parmesan cheese evenly over the fork-marked pastry base. Spread the cooled onion filling over the cheese and scatter the artichoke hearts and olives on top.

5. Time to Bake: Carefully lift the tart by the edges of the foil and slide onto the hot cookie sheet. Bake for 30 minutes until puffy, crisp and golden brown. Garnish with chopped thyme.
Yield: 1 8-inch tart

THYMELY TIP
If you suddenly realize that you have erred in one step of this recipe and feel it absolutely necessary to travel back in time to correct it, don't get carried away and alter the course of gastronomic history. You just might return to find tonight's menu changed to corndogs and Jell-O.™ Bon Appetite!

INSIDE SCOOP
Eric Stoltz was originally cast as Marty McFly.

Dearly Departed Sole

Beetlejuice
(1988)

Does death scare you? Calm down, there's nothing to be afraid of. In *Beetlejuice* we learn that the dead can be cute and friendly and even kind of sexy—as long as they're played by Geena Davis and Alec Baldwin. It's our mission with this recipe to show you that fish and beets don't have to be scary either. Prepared our way they can be savory and delicious and, like Geena and Alec, kind of sexy. So dive in, and if you feel afraid, just repeat after us: Beets are delicious, beets are delicious, beets are delicious . . .

Chew on This

We had to do some "sole" searching for this one, but, after haunting our local fish market, we found that true sole is about as rare as being raised from the dead. Presumably most of what is sold as sole in the U.S. is actually Cousin Flounder, not just a sole substitute but a flavorful fish in its own right.

For the Beet sauce:
5-6 medium beets, greens intact
3 cloves garlic, peeled
3 Tbsp lemon juice
1 Tbsp rice wine vinegar
Salt and pepper

> "Oh what food
> these morsels be."
> —Glenn "Otho" Shadix

For the Sole:
4 large sole filets
Salt and freshly ground black pepper
2 Tbsp butter, softened
Zest of 1 lemon and 1 orange
1 cup bone-dry white wine
1 "Handbook for the Recently Deceased"

1. **"Has being dead got you down?"** Well friends, you've come to the right recipe! Wash the beets well, then cut off the beet greens about 2 inches from the base.

2. Place the beets and garlic cloves in a pot; cover with cold water and bring to a boil—until tender. Reduce the heat and simmer, uncovered, for 30-45 minutes.

3. Dip the beet greens one by one in the boiling water until limp (about 15 seconds). Trim off any thick stems and lay the wilted greens out flat on a towel.

4. **Beetsauce! Beetsauce! Beetsauce!:** When the beets can be easily pierced with a fork, peel under running water and cut into

quarters. Then place the beets, garlic cloves, 1/2 cup of the cooking liquid and the lemon juice in a blender and process until smooth. Transfer the mixture to a small saucepan and place over low heat; season to taste with rice wine vinegar, salt and pepper.

5. Preheat oven to 425°F.

6. Search Your Sole: Lightly spread the tops of each sole filet with butter, then season with citrus zest, salt and black pepper to taste.

7. Wrap the filets individually in beet greens (to resemble cozy little mummies), then transfer to a greased baking dish and moisten with white wine. Cover loosely with foil and bake anywhere from 10 minutes to an eternity, whichever comes first.

8. It's Showtime! Serve over a ghastly, but tasty pool of beet sauce, garnish with freshly manifested ectoplasm (or a little lemon zest) and eat as though it's your last meal.

9. Summon help with the dishes from beyond. Lure any guests—living or dead—into the kitchen with a rousing chorus of "Day-O," and hope someone offers to release you from the torment of "Dirty Dish Purgatory."
Yield: 4 servings

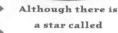

Food for Thought

Although there is a star called "Betelgeuse," apparently it has nothing to do with Michael Keaton's character in *Beetlejuice*. "Betelgeuse" does have a cool translation, though. In Arabic it means "the armpit of the giant."

INSIDE SCOOP

Tim Burton's first big project, the half-hour cartoon, "Frankenweenie," was shelved by Disney because it was considered too violent for children. Luckily Warner Brothers was looking for someone to direct real-life cartoon Pee-Wee Herman and hired Burton to helm *Pee-Wee's Big Adventure*. Burton has gone on to direct some of our favorite films, including *Edward Scissorhands* and *Ed Wood*.

Napoleon "Bone-Apart" Snapper Sandwiches

Even though Napoleon is given credit for this sandwich, it was Bill and Ted who turned him on to the most excellent potato-chip crust. Cook on, dudes!

For the Bone-Apart Snapper:
4 6-oz snapper filets, skinned, boned and ready to party
1/2 cup heavy cream
2 cups barbecued potato chips, finely ground (like dust in the wind, dude)
2 Tbsp peanut oil
4 excellent French rolls

For the Tartar Sauce:
1/2 cup mayonnaise
1 tsp capers
3 Tbsp sweet pickles, diced
1 scallion, finely chopped
1 Tbsp freshly squeezed lemon juice
1/8 tsp freshly ground black pepper

For the Rest of the Tasty Toppings:
1 cup red onion, thinly sliced
3 cups iceberg lettuce, shredded
1/4 cup fresh dill, coarsely chopped
2-3 Tbsp pickled jalapeño, sliced (retain juice)
2 ripe tomatoes, sliced
1 exceptionally loud musical instrument of any type
  (no actual proficiency required)

1. Prep the Filets, Dude: Preheat oven to 450°F. Rinse the snapper filets in cold water and blot dry with paper towels. Place in a bowl, cover with the cream, and refrigerate 10 minutes.

2. Pour 1 cup of the ground potato chips into a shallow baking dish just large enough to accommodate the filets. Remove the snapper from the cream and lay side by side over the ground chips. Sprinkle the remaining potato chips evenly over the filets and cover with plastic wrap. Press the coating firmly into the fish with a spatula and refrigerate for 15 minutes, while making the tartar sauce.

3. Totally make the Tartar Sauce: Combine the mayonnaise with the capers, sweet pickle and scallion. Stir in the lemon juice and season with black pepper.

4. Look Out for the Iceberg, Dude!: In a medium bowl, combine the shredded iceberg, sliced onion, chopped dill and the jalapeños with their juice. Toss and refrigerate. Preheat oven to 450°F.

5. Get Totally Crispy: Heat 2 tablespoons of peanut oil in a large cast-iron skillet over medium-high heat. Place the coated filets in the hot pan and cook for 2 minutes, without turning. Transfer skillet to the hot oven and continue cooking uncovered for 8 minutes. Place the French rolls in the oven to toast during the last 2 minutes of cooking time.

6. Time for Munchies, Dude: Pile copious amounts of tartar sauce, tomatoes and spicy iceberg on each roll, top with the snapper and chow down.

7. Gnarly Philosophical Tip: Always remember, dudes, the most awesome way to be excellent to each other is through the righteous and timely preparation of totally succulent munchies.
Yield: 4 excellent servings

Chew on This

Genghis Khan never ate off a plate at home like he does in this movie.

INSIDE SCOOP

Scores of different fish are sold under the name red snapper. Most of them are mild, white-fleshed fish that wouldn't be easy to sell under their real names. (Bill & Ted's Blubberlip Sandwiches?)

Young-and-Naked Fish Kabobs with Mango Tiki Sauce

The Blue Lagoon
(1980)

Light the torches, sharpen your spears, and dive into the tropical innocence of a dinner that can be made with virtually no modern tools or restrictive clothing.

For the Mango Tiki Sauce:

2 medium mangos, peeled and cut in chunks,
   or 1 cup frozen mango
2 Tbsp soy sauce
4 Tbsp dry sherry
1/4 cup brown sugar
1/4 cup cider vinegar
1 Tbsp peanut oil
2 cloves garlic, peeled and thinly sliced
2 tsp fresh ginger, grated
1/4 medium white onion, thinly sliced

For the Young-and-Naked Kabobs:

1-2 lbs mahi-mahi (if unavailable, substitute swordfish,
   shark, or fresh tuna)
2 small zucchini
1 red onion
2 bell peppers
1/2 fresh pineapple
2 firm, ripe papayas
3 Tbsp olive oil
Salt and pepper
2 scallions, thinly sliced on the diagonal
1 skimpy loincloth
1 roll Scotch tape (to affix long hair modestly to "bumpies")

1. Mango Tiki Sauce: In the bowl of a food processor or blender, combine the mango, soy sauce, sherry, brown sugar, and cider vinegar; blend to a smooth puree.

Chew on This

MANGO TIP #34

One way to tell if a mango is ripe is the presence of oozing or weeping near the stem. If this condition exists on anything but your mango, there's a strong possibility that more than two of you are on the island.

2. Heat the peanut oil in a medium saucepan over medium heat. Add the garlic, ginger, and onion and stir fry for 1 minute (being careful not to burn the mixture). Add the pureed mango mixture and bring to a boil. Reduce heat and simmer for 10 minutes. Thin with a little island springwater if desired.

3. Kabob Construction: Preheat broiler (the part of the stove you rarely use and are probably storing lids in). Pretend you are Christopher Atkins, spearfishing in clear, tropical waters, while Brooke waits shyly in the hut. Using separate bowls to hold each item: cut the mahi-mahi into 2-inch chunks; cut the zucchini, red onion, bell peppers, pineapple, and papayas into 1-inch pieces; leave cherry tomatoes whole.

4. Spear kabob ingredients in sequence until each skewer is loaded with colorful trophies. Brush lightly with olive oil, season with salt and pepper, and place on a foil-lined broiler tray.

5. Broil the kabobs for a total of 10 minutes, rotating a few times to brown evenly. For the last minute of cooking, brush on a little of the mango tiki sauce. When done, arrange the fish kabobs on a platter (or banana leaf) and spoon sauce over the top. Garnish with scallions and start the luau.
Yield: 4 servings

SKEWER TIP #8
Keep your skewers from burning up during broiling by first soaking them in water.

INSIDE SCOOP
Employ the spent and empty skewers as your own form of currency to barter favor from your fellow castaways. Or better yet, get them to do the dishes. Aloha!

Food for Thought

Question: Where was the lipstick tree? Answer: Right next to the blow-dryer bush.

Blue Steel
(1990)

We're not shooting our mouth off. The flavor of these high caliber shells is positively arresting. Your dinner guests will put their hands up for more . . . then be sure to reload.

1/4 cup kosher salt
2 lbs eggplant
1/2 cup olive oil
1 small onion, peeled and sliced thin
4 cloves garlic, peeled and minced
3 cups, or 1 28-oz can tomatoes, peeled, seeded and chopped
1 lb Conchiglie, or shell-shaped pasta
1/2 cup ricotta cheese
1/2 cup basil, freshly chopped
4 cups baby spinach
Red pepper flakes,
Salt and freshly ground black pepper, to taste
Freshly grated Parmesan cheese
1 figure enhancing, bulletproof Wondervest

1. Peel the eggplant and cut into 2-inch cubes. Place the eggplant in a colander, sprinkle with salt and set in the sink to drain for at least 20 minutes.

2. Rinse the eggplant well to remove the salt, then place in a clean, dry towel and squeeze out as much water as possible.

3. Put 5-6 quarts of lightly salted water in a large pot, bring to a boil.

4. Heat a large sauté pan with half of the olive oil until quite hot and sauté the eggplant until tender. Remove eggplant from the pan and drain on paper towels.

5. Add the remaining olive oil and sauté the onion over medium heat until golden brown, then add the garlic and cook another 30 seconds or so. Add the chopped tomatoes, increase the heat to medium high and cook 10 minutes.

6. Meanwhile, add the pasta to the boiling water and stir immediately to

Chew on This

At last count there were over 600 shapes of pasta available in the world. One pound of pasta generally serves 4 people.

prevent sticking. Cover the pot until the water returns to a boil, then uncover and cook according to package instructions (or a little less for *al dente*), stirring often.

7. Add the eggplant cubes to the sauce and reduce the heat to low.

8. Drain the pasta into a colander over a large pasta bowl (this heats up the bowl nicely), carefully pour the hot water out and wipe the bowl dry.

9. Combine the pasta, sauce, ricotta, basil and spinach in the warm bowl and toss together. Season to taste with freshly ground black pepper, red pepper flakes and Parmesan cheese.

10. Set the table and invite a new friend to join you for dinner (making sure to perform a thorough background check first).
Yield: 4 servings

ROLL OUT THE RED CARPET!

The daughter of Hollywood royalty Janet Leigh and Tony Curtis, Jamie Leigh Curtis is married to actual British royalty. Her husband, actor/director Christopher Guest (*Spinal Tap* and *Waiting For Guffman*) is "Lord Haden-Guest," and Jamie, by marriage, is "Lady Haden-Guest."

INSIDE SCOOP

Both tomatoes and eggplant are considered fruits, not vegetables, and belong to the nightshade family. The Italian word for eggplant, *melezana*, is derived from the Latin word meaning "unhealthy apple" and eggplant was originally believed to bring about instant insanity, epilepsy or uncontrollable deviant sexual behavior. So next time you're in trouble with the law, you might want to try the babaganoush defense. (Not so far-fetched—it worked for Twinkies.)

Funky Chicken

**The Blues
Brothers**
(1980)

It's ten feet to the kitchen, we have a fryer full of oil, a bag of chicken, it's night, and we're wearing chef's hats.

For the Buttermilk Marinade:
8 garlic cloves, finely chopped
1 tsp fresh thyme, chopped
1 Tbsp Tabasco sauce
3 cups buttermilk
1 cup ice

For the Coating:
3 cups all-purpose flour
1/2 cup cornmeal
2 tsp black pepper
2 tsp salt
1 Tbsp paprika

For the Funky Chicken:
Canola oil, as needed
1 large scoop soul (or soul substitute)
**8 chicken thighs, boned (feel free to substitute white meat
    if desired; you can always pretend it's dark)**

1. Mix together the garlic, thyme, oregano, Tabasco, buttermilk, and ice.

2. Cover the chicken with the buttermilk mixture and refrigerate.

3. In a large, shallow dish, combine the flour, cornmeal, black pepper, salt, and paprika.

4. Fill a large, heavy skillet with canola oil to a depth of 1/2-1 inch. Place the pan over medium-high heat. If using an electric frying pan, set the temperature anywhere from 360°F to 370°F.

5. Check the temperature by dropping a cube of bread into the oil; it should take about a minute to brown.

6. Remove chicken from the buttermilk and dredge each piece in the flour mixture; shake off the excess. Dip again into the buttermilk, then one last time into the flour. If working with limited counter space, pour

Food for Thought

When breading the
chicken pieces, use
only one hand in
case you get a phone
call from your
agent.

—Annabelle Gurwitch,
Host of "Dinner &
a Movie"

the flour mixture into a paper bag, place chicken pieces in one at a time and shake.

7. Lay that funky chicken down into the hot oil without crowding or touching. Frying too many pieces at once will cause the oil to cool and the chicken will end up greasy. Fry each piece for a total of 20-25 minutes, turning often.

8. If frying more than one batch of chicken, keep cooked pieces warm on a baking sheet in a 250°F oven.

9. FUNKY TIP: You can be the Godfather of Soul Food! After wowing your guests with one funky dish after another, drape your sweat-soaked apron over your shoulders like a cape and have someone lead you dramatically out of the kitchen. (For added effect, mop your forehead while declaring, "I can't cook no mo'.") Do this between each course until it's time to do the dishes, then disappear completely.
Yield: 4 servings

INSIDE SCOOP

You can't throw a chicken bone without hitting a famous musician in this movie. Watch out for:

- Steve Lawrence
- James Brown
- Aretha Franklin
- Ray Charles
- Cab Calloway
- Donald "Duck" Dunne
- Willie "Too Big" Hall
- John Lee Hooker
- Chaka Khan

Breakfast Club Sandwich

The Breakfast Club
(1985)

Finally—a sandwich that understands your desperate need for individuality. Who cares what the adults say, they don't listen to you anyway. You can have a sandwich for breakfast on a Friday night if you want to. Remember, we're all in this together.

You Will Need (But What About My Needs?):
4 slices thick-cut bacon, salty as one's own tears
1 tsp freshly cracked black pepper
1 Tbsp butter
1 Tbsp onion, finely chopped
1/4 cup red bell pepper, thinly sliced
2 large eggs, beaten
Salt and pepper
1 tsp fresh basil, very thinly sliced
3 Tbsp mozzarella, grated
3 thick slices sourdough bread
3 Tbsp mayonnaise
1/2 avocado, sliced
1 ripe tomato, sliced
1 handful watercress
Self-pity, to taste

Food for Thought

EGG TIP #879

If uncertain as to whether or not an egg is fresh, lower it into salted water to cover.
If it floats, it's probably time to buy new eggs.

1. Preheat oven to 375°F. While the oven heats up, so can you. Take a few minutes to whine about anything that your parents ever did or didn't do that might have stunted your emotional or spiritual growth.

2. Lay bacon out on a cookie sheet and sprinkle with the cracked black pepper. Bake for 10-15 minutes until crisp, turning once. Remove from oven and set aside. (Leave oven on.)

3. **To Make Frittata:** Melt butter in a small non-stick sauté pan over medium heat. When the butter begins to bubble, add the onion and bell pepper and sauté until tender, about one minute.

4. Pour the beaten eggs into the center of the hot pan. Cook for a minute without stirring to let the sides and bottom set. Using a spatula or fork, pull the cooked egg away from the sides while tilting the pan to

let any raw egg run down to the hot bottom. Season the frittata with salt, pepper, and fresh basil and top with grated mozzarella. Transfer the pan to the hot oven and bake for 3 minutes.

5. Remove crusts from bread if desired (depending upon which character you most identify with) and toast lightly.

6. Set out the remaining ingredients and begin constructing the sandwich from the bottom up: Start with one slice of toast and spread mayonnaise on one side. Add the frittata and the avocado slices. Spread both sides of the second piece of toast with a little mayo and lay that over the avocado. Layer the peppered bacon, tomato slices, and watercress. Spread the last, but no less important, piece of toast with a little mayonnaise and place firmly, but sensitively, over that bitter and often misunderstood watercress.

7. Viciously spear the layers together at each corner with toothpicks to vent any remaining teenage aggression. Cut diagonally into quarters and remember that, like all of us, each quarter contains a little bit of everything . . . .
Yield: 2 servings

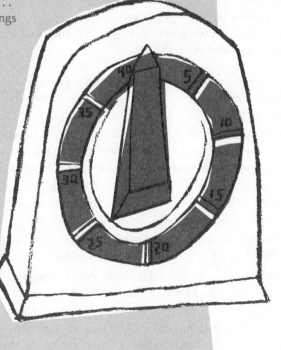

Chew on This

This is not a "heart smart" meal, so you'll need to get your exercise. Try doing what Emilio Estevez does in the movie: Run through your local high school library pumping your fists in the air. Do it for 20 minutes daily or until the librarian throws you out.

INSIDE SCOOP

Writer/Director John Hughes based *The Breakfast Club* on his own high school experience including numerous stays in morning detention.

"Rolling in Dough"
Homemade Ballpark Pretzels

What would you do with $30 million dollars? We'd stock up on a lifetime supply of these classic ballpark treats.

1 1/4 cups lukewarm water
1 tsp sugar
1 Tbsp active dry yeast
1 1/2 tsp salt
4 cups unbleached, all-purpose flour
1 Tbsp olive oil
4 tsp baking soda
1 quart water
1 egg, beaten with 2 tsp water
Kosher salt, whole cumin, caraway, sesame and poppy seeds
Plenty of tax deductions

1. Combine the water, sugar and yeast in a large mixing bowl and set aside in a warm spot. After 10-15 minutes, the mixture should begin to foam and bubble.

2. Add the salt and half of the flour and mix well with a wooden spoon. Turn the dough out onto a clean, floured surface and gradually knead in the remaining flour to form a smooth and elastic dough.

3. Continue to knead the dough for another 5 minutes before transferring to a clean bowl oiled with a few drops of olive oil. Turn the dough in the bowl to coat all sides evenly with oil.

4. Cover the bowl with a clean kitchen towel or plastic wrap and set in a warm, draft-free place until doubled in bulk, about 45 minutes.

5. Preheat the oven to 450°F. Punch the dough down and roll into a large log. Divide into 12 even pieces, then roll each piece into a 16-18 inch rope.

6. Shape the pretzels into dollar signs, baseball bats or any other shapes that come to mind. To form a traditional pretzel shape, simply tie

Chew on This

According to our sources, the word "pretzel" is from the Italian "pretiola" meaning "little reward." As early as 600 A.D., monks would bake bits of scrap bread dough as a reward to children who learned their prayers. The shape was intended to resemble the arms of a child folded across her chest in prayer.

the dough into a loose knot pinching the loose ends across the loops.

7. Combine the baking soda and water in a small saucepan and bring to a boil. Using a slotted spoon, carefully lower each pretzel in the boiling water until it begins to float, about 30 seconds.

8. Drain each pretzel and transfer to a greased baking sheet, brush lightly with the egg-water mixture and sprinkle generously with kosher salt, cumin, caraway, sesame and poppy seeds.

9. Cover the pretzels with a cloth and allow to rise again, about 5 minutes.

10. Bake in preheated 450°F oven for about 15 minutes or until golden brown. Serve hot with plenty of cold beer and mustard.

11. Remember to save room for a frozen asset snow cone or some legal tender chicken tenders.

Yield: 1 dozen pretzels

INSIDE SCOOP

Here's a reassuring thought: Your odds of winning the lottery actually ARE better than your odds of getting struck by lightning.

Although Monty Brewster squandered his inheritance, one study of lottery winners reports that they're actually cautious with their newfound riches:

- 80 % buy a new vehicle
- 70 % seek financial counseling
- 60 % take a vacation
- 60 % pay off debt
- 60 % give to charity
- 50 % buy a new house
- 50 % retire or quit their jobs
- 30 % keep their jobs
- 15 % find new jobs

Classic Cul-de-Sac Mac 'N Cheese

. . . or as we like to call it, Dr. Klopeck's What's-That-Smell-in-the-Basement Hackaroni Casserole.

For the Cheese Sauce:
3 cups whole milk
1/2 onion
1 bay leaf
2 whole cloves
1/2 cup butter
1/4 cup shallots, minced
1/3 cup flour
1 tsp dry mustard
1/8 tsp white pepper
1 Tbsp Worcestershire sauce
1/8 tsp nutmeg
1/8 tsp cayenne
1 tsp fresh thyme, chopped
1/2 tsp salt

For the Filling:
16 oz dry macaroni
1 1/2 cups Gruyere or Swiss cheese, grated
2 cups cheddar cheese, grated
1 1/2 cups Parmesan cheese, grated
1/2 cup bread crumbs
1 "Kiss the Cook" apron
1 set lawn darts
1 box of grass seed
1 dirty little secret

Chew on This

Tom Hanks was the first actor to win back-to-back Academy Awards™ for Best Actor since Spencer Tracy did it in 1937 and 1938. Hanks won for *Philadelphia* and *Forrest Gump*.

Food for Thought

Suburbs began in the 1800s when improvements in transportation allowed people to live farther away from their work.

1. Preheat the oven to 375°F. Butter a 3-quart casserole.

2. Cook the macaroni *al dente* (a minute or two less than the package instructions). Rinse in cold water, drain, and set aside.

3. Make the Cheese Sauce: Pour the milk into a small saucepan. Tack the bay leaf to the onion with the cloves and place in the milk. Slowly bring the milk to a simmer over medium-low heat.

4. Melt 1/2 of the butter in a medium saucepan over medium heat. Add the chopped shallots and cook until soft. Add the flour, dry mustard, and white pepper and cook another 3 minutes, stirring often.

5. Slowly add the hot milk to the butter and flour mixture, whisking constantly. Stir in the Worcestershire; transfer the clove-studded onion and simmer at least 20 minutes (stirring occasionally), until sauce is thick and creamy.

6. Remove from heat, discard the onion, and stir in 1/2 cup each of the grated cheddar and Gruyere. Whisk in the fresh thyme, nutmeg, cayenne, and salt.

7. Mix and Bake: Turn the cooked, drained macaroni into the buttered casserole, add the hot cheese sauce, and stir together. Stir in 1/2 cup of the Parmesan and the remaining cheddar and Gruyere.

8. Sprinkle with the rest of the Parmesan cheese and the bread crumbs; dot with the remaining butter and bake uncovered in the upper third of the oven for 30 minutes, or until brown and bubbly.
Yield: 8 servings

INSIDE SCOOP
CHEESE FACT #73
Legend has it that the first cheese probably was made by accident. In the Middle East, milk was commonly stored in bags made from animal intestines, which naturally contain rennet, the enzyme responsible for separating milk into curds and whey.

Carrie's Prom Crisp

Carrie
(1976)

They're not "all gonna laugh at you!" They're not "all gonna laugh at you!" And you can bet they'll ask for seconds.

For the Fruit Filling:
5-6 Fuji or Granny Smith apples (about 6 cups when sliced)
2 Tbsp fresh lemon juice
1 1/2 pints strawberries, hulled and quartered
2-3 Tbsp sugar, depending on sweetness of the fruit
1 Tbsp all-purpose flour
1 tsp vanilla

For the Crisp Topping:
1 cup walnuts
1 cup all-purpose flour
1/2 cup light brown sugar
2 Tbsp white sugar
1/3 cup oatmeal
1 1/2 tsp cinnamon
1/2 cup cold butter, cut into 1/4-inch pieces
15 gallons pig blood, well aged

1. Sit perfectly still in a comfortable chair. Using only the untapped power of your impassioned epicurean mind, will the razor-sharp knife to peel, core, and thinly slice the fleshy fruit of the apples in a macabre dance of flashing steel and flying peel. Preheat the oven to 350°F and grease a 10-12-inch cast-iron skillet with butter.

2. For the Filling: Toss fruit slices with lemon juice to prevent darkening. In a large mixing bowl, combine the vanilla, sugars, and flour. Add the apples and strawberries and toss gently to mix, being careful not to break apart the apple slices.

3. For the Crisp Topping: Lay walnut pieces on a cookie sheet and toast for 10 minutes in the 350°F oven. Cool and chop viciously into small pieces.

4. In a medium mixing bowl combine the flour, sugars, oatmeal, and cinnamon. Add the walnuts and stir together. Work the butter pieces into

Chew on This

Fruit Crisps are easy to make and hard to ruin. Although we used apples and strawberries, try experimenting with seasonal fruits and other types of nuts.

the topping mixture a little at a time with your fingers or a pastry blender. Continue blending until the topping holds together and crumbles to the size of small peas.

5. Assembly: Pour the fruit filling evenly into the buttered skillet. Distribute the topping over the filling, pressing down lightly.

6. Fire Drill: Put the skillet in the hot oven. Slam and lock the oven door. Walk slowly out into the night. (Make sure to return in 40-45 minutes to find the topping brown and crunchy and the glistening crimson juices beginning to bubble up and ooze from the surface.) Eat without mercy.

Yield: 6-8 servings

INSIDE SCOOP

Carrie Fisher was originally set to play the lead role in *Carrie*, but she refused to do the nude scenes. She eventually switched roles with Sissy Spacek who had been cast in a little film then in development, called *Star Wars*.

Scrooge's Turkey Legs with Crispy Gruel Stuffing

A Christmas Carol
(1938)

Here at "Dinner & a Movie" we have certain traditions. When we watch *A Christmas Carol*, we need to be sliding the turkey legs into the oven the moment we hear, "Marley was dead. Dead as a doornail"; basting at "Bah, humbug!"; and if all goes well, dining with the Cratchits when we hear Tiny Tim utter, "God bless us, every one!" Hey, it's just something we do. This year, why not start the tradition at your house?

For Scrooge's Turkey Legs:
3 large onions, peeled and sliced in 1/2-inch rings
1 Tbsp garlic, peeled and minced
4 Tbsp olive oil
6 turkey drumsticks, on sale if possible
Salt and pepper

For the Crispy Gruel Stuffing:
1/4 cup vermouth
1/2 cup golden raisins
8 oz pork sausage
1 onion, chopped
1 cup celery, chopped
2 Granny Smith apples, peeled, cored, and chopped
1 1/2 cups gruel (dry oatmeal)
3 cups dried bread cubes
1 cup walnut pieces
1/2 cup chicken broth
1 egg, beaten
1 tsp ground sage
1/4 cup fresh parsley, chopped
1/2 tsp freshly ground black pepper
4 oz (1/2 stick) melted butter
1 set of chains, forged in life, to be worn eternally

Chew on This

Although our recipe calls for drumsticks, most turkeys are raised for maximum production of white meat. It's not uncommon for their breasts to get so big that they can't get near enough to reach each other to mate.

1. Roast the Legs: Preheat oven to 350°F. Brush the onion slices with a little olive oil and lay side by side in a shallow roasting pan. Combine the garlic with the remaining olive oil and rub onto the drumsticks. Season with salt and pepper.

2. Arrange the turkey legs over the onion slices and place pan in the lower third of the oven. Roast for a total of 90 minutes. (The stuffing goes in the oven during the last 45 minutes of cooking.) Occasionally baste both the stuffing and the legs with any accumulated pan juices.

3. Make the Stuffing: Put the raisins into a small saucepan, cover with vermouth and bring to a simmer. Remove from the heat and set aside.

4. In a large skillet over medium heat, lightly brown the sausage, breaking it up as it cooks. Use a slotted spoon to transfer sausage to a large mixing bowl and set aside. Add the onion and celery to the skillet and cook until softened. Stir in the chopped apples and cook 15 minutes, stirring often. Add the raisins and vermouth, increase the heat to high, and cook until most of the liquid has evaporated. Scrape the hot mixture into the mixing bowl containing the sausage, stir together, and cool to room temperature.

5. Fold in 1 cup oatmeal, 2 cups bread cubes, 1/2 cup walnuts, chicken broth, and the beaten egg. Season with sage, parsley, and black pepper and mix together well. Turn the mixture into a well-buttered shallow casserole or baking dish, sprinkle the remaining gruel, bread cubes and walnuts evenly over the top and drizzle with melted butter. Bake for 45 minutes.

6. On a single dinner plate, balance all six turkey legs atop the pile of now caramelized onions, surrounded by a ring of crispy gruel stuffing. Eat every bite yourself. Don your night-cap, climb into bed, and see which shows up first: the Ghost of Christmas Past or the Pain of Heartburn Present.
Yield: 4-6 servings (or 1 miser)

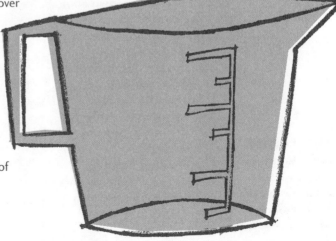

Edible Fruitcake...
No, Really!

A Christmas Story (1983)

Hey, hey, hey, wait a minute, before you turn the page . . . You should know that this fruitcake has been designed to be less dense than the traditional, family heirloom, brandy-soaked, half-life of plutonium, door-stopper kind of fruit cake. It actually can be enjoyed warm, out of the oven if desired.

For the "Fruit" Part:
1 1/2 cups dried apricots, diced into 1/2-inch chunks
1 1/2 cups dried cranberries
1 1/2 cups golden raisins
1 cup pineapple, diced into 1/2-inch chunks
1/4 cup Gran Marnier
1 cup pecans, coarsely chopped
1 cup blanched almonds,
   coarsely chopped

For the "Cake" Part:
2 sticks butter, softened
1/2 cup light brown sugar
1 cup confectioner's sugar
Zest of 1 lemon, grated
Zest of 2 oranges
   or tangerines, grated
6 eggs, separated
2 tsp vanilla extract
1/2 tsp almond extract
2 1/2 cups all-purpose flour
1/2 tsp salt
1 tsp baking powder
2 tsp ground cinnamon
1/2 tsp ground nutmeg
1/4 tsp ground ginger
1 leg of lamp

FRUITCAKE CONFIDENTIAL

We must admit that prior to tracing the roots of the modern, joke-butted fruitcake, we were all too ready to place the blame squarely on the stiff shoulders of the English. We apologize. It seems for centuries these festive depth charges have existed simultaneously and been thrust annually upon the unsuspecting in Germany, Italy, Mexico, Ireland . . . oh, and of course . . . England.

INSIDE SCOOP

This film was based on an autobio-graphical story by American humorist Jean Shepherd.

1. Preheat oven to 250°F. Butter 2 9x5-inch loaf pans and line bottoms with parchment paper or aluminum foil. Butter the paper or foil and set aside.

2. In a medium mixing bowl, combine the apricots, cranberries, golden raisins, pineapple, and Gran Marnier; stir well and set aside. In another mixing bowl, sift together the flour, salt, baking powder, cinnamon, nutmeg, and ginger. Add the chopped nuts and toss a few times.

3. In a large mixing bowl, cream together the brown sugar, confectioner's sugar, and butter until fluffy and smooth. Blend in the egg yolks, one at a time, allowing each to incorporate before adding the next. Stir in the vanilla, almond extract, lemon zest, and orange zest.

4. To the butter mixture, alternately fold in the flour mixture and the fruit mixture; stir until well blended. Beat the egg whites until soft peaks begin to form. Fold the beaten egg whites a third at a time, into the batter.

5. Pour half of the batter into each of the prepared pans, filling them no more than 1 inch from the top. Smooth out the tops and bake about 2 hours. To check for doneness, insert a knife or skewer in the center. If the knife emerges clean, cake is cooked. Remove from oven and cool in the pans for 30 minutes, turn out, and brush the tops and sides with a little Gran Marnier. Eat warm, or wrap tightly in plastic wrap and refrigerate.

6. Note: If what you want is a fruitcake that can withstand the ravages of time better than yourself, double the Gran Marnier and add at least two cups of brandy or rum to the dried fruit. Soak for 24 hours before proceeding with recipe. (The next thing to do is decide who in the family is worthy of inheriting these durable, fruity monoliths.)
Yield: Two 9-inch loaves

Food for Thought

Want to turn your next ill-advised winter pole-licking dare into a party? Try our version: the refreshing "Fruity Frozen Flagpole." Just pour your favorite fruit juice on a frozen outdoor pole and watch the fun. We feel that since your tongue will be painfully stuck to the pole for a long while, it should at least taste good. Your guests will never want to leave! . . . Well, they can't.

Butcher Holler Ham Hocks and Collards

(To be sung to the tune of "Coal Miner's Daughter")
This recipe was born from a coal miner's table.
You watched it on "Dinner & a Movie" if you've got cable . . .

1 Tbsp butter or olive oil
6 cloves garlic, peeled and crushed
3 smoked ham hocks (about 2 pounds)
1-2 quarts water or chicken stock
2 lbs collard greens
2 quarts water plus 1 Tbsp salt
4 cups fresh or frozen black-eyed peas
1 tsp freshly ground black pepper
1/2 tsp red pepper flakes
1 tsp fresh thyme, chopped
2 tsp brown sugar
1 Tbsp cider vinegar
The desire to make it big . . . as big as your hair

1. Heat the oil or butter in a large, heavy saucepan over a medium heat. Add the garlic and ham hocks and sauté until golden brown.

2. Cover with water or chicken stock and bring to a boil. Reduce heat and simmer 45 minutes to an hour.

3. While the hocks simmer, wash the greens thoroughly and remove the toughest part of the stems.

4. Bring 2 quarts lightly salted water to a boil in a large pot. Add the greens, stir and cover; cook about 2 minutes, then drain in a colander.

5. Rinse greens with cold water to stop the greens from cooking. Squeeze out excess water and chop coarsely. Set aside.

6. When the ham hocks begin to tender up some, take them out and pull off all the meat you can, chop it up and add it back.

7. Give the bones to the dogs.

INSIDE SCOOP

Born in Butcher Holler, Kentucky, Loretta Lynn got married when she was 13 but didn't hit it big on the country scene until she was 29. Lynn handpicked Sissy Spacek to portray her in this film.

8. Add the black-eyed peas, black pepper, red pepper flakes, thyme, brown sugar, cider vinegar and collards. Continue cooking at a simmer for about 20 minutes. Adjust seasonings to taste and serve with hot, buttered cornbread.

9. Pick the biggest hussy at the table and tell her that she's not only woman enough, but actually welcome to, take your man as long as she does the dishes first.

Yield: 4 servings

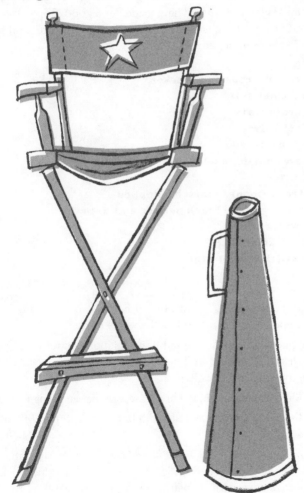

Chew on This

Tradition requires Southerners to eat black-eyed peas, preferably with greens, on New Year's Day for good fortune in the coming year. No one is definite about the origins of this ritual, but legend has it that it will ensure money in your pocket all year long. The black-eyed peas symbolize coins and greens symbolize paper money.

Food for Thought

The black-eyed pea is really a bean.

Triple Axel Rotisserie Chicken

If you think Nancy Kerrigan suffered, see what D.B. Sweeney goes through as the poor, but honest, skating partner to rich-girl champion Moira Kelly. Maybe D.B. should have made her a good "Triple Axel Rotisserie Chicken." It's guaranteed to sweep any ice princess off her feet. No Zamboni® required.

- 1 (3 1/2 to 4 lb) roasting chicken
- 3/4 cup kosher salt
- 3 quarts cold water
- 1 cup black olives
- 1 lemon, quartered
- 10-15 cloves garlic, peeled and crushed
- 3 Tbsp butter
- 1 sprig fresh thyme, coarsely chopped
- Salt, freshly ground black pepper and paprika
- 1/2 cup white wine
- 1/2 cup chicken stock
- 1 big guy with a steel pipe

Chew on This

After a knee injury ended his dream of playing professional baseball, D.B. Sweeney turned to acting, where, lo and behold, he often plays characters with athletic backgrounds.

1. Preheat the oven to 475°F. Mix the kosher salt and the water in a bowl large enough to accommodate the whole chicken.

2. Submerge the chicken in the salt brine solution and refrigerate for anywhere from 30 minutes to 2 hours (depending on how much time you have, the longer, the juicier).

3. While the chicken soaks in the brine, prepare the remaining ingredients.

4. Rinse the chicken inside and out with hot water and dry well with paper towels.

5. Season the cavity liberally with salt and black pepper, then stuff with the olives, lemon and crushed garlic. Tie the ends of the drumsticks together very loosely with kitchen twine to partially seal the cavity.

6. Combine the thyme and butter in a small saucepan over low heat. When the butter has melted, remove the pan from the heat.

7. Brush the skin with the melted thyme-butter mixture and season with salt, black pepper and paprika.

8. Place a rack over a roasting pan larger than the chicken to be roasted. Arrange the chicken on one side of the rack and place in the oven. Set a timer for 20 minutes.

9. When the timer sounds, turn the bird onto its other side (don't drop it or you'll lose points), brush with melted butter and reduce the oven temperature to 350°F. Set the timer again for 20 minutes.

10. This time when the timer goes off, turn the chicken breast-side up, brush with the remaining melted butter and roast for an additional 15 minutes. Check the internal temperature with an instant-read thermometer inserted in the thickest part of the thigh. It should register from 165°F-170, if not, continue roasting another 10 minutes and check again. When the chicken is fully cooked, transfer to a cutting board or platter and let rest 10-15 minutes before carving.

11. Spoon off and discard most of the rendered fat from the roasting pan. Add the white wine and chicken stock and place over a medium-high heat, scraping the bottom of the pan with a wooden spoon or Zamboni® to loosen any tasty browned bits. Cook down until syrupy and spoon over the portions along with the olives and garlic from inside the bird.

12. Tip: If anytime during the meal, anyone brushes against you even accidentally, remember to clutch yourself and dramatically wail, "Why Me?" (odds are you'll get out of doing the dishes). Yield: 4 servings

INSIDE SCOOP

Professional chefs know that soaking a whole chicken or turkey in a salt-water solution before roasting helps retain a significant amount of moisture in the finished bird.

D.O.A.
(1981)

Biscuits to Die For (with One Foot in the Gravy)

What would you do if you found out you had 24 hours to live? We'd cook up some Biscuits to Die For with One Foot in the Gravy. With plenty of butter, cream, shortening and sausage this dish is deadly delicious and would be a great last meal.

For the Gravy:
1 lb country sausage
1 red onion, minced
1 cup mushrooms, sliced
3 Tbsp flour
2 cups chicken stock
1/2 cup cream (optional)
1 tsp fresh thyme, chopped
salt and freshly ground
  black pepper, to taste
Tabasco sauce, to taste

For the Biscuits:
4 cups self-rising flour
3 Tbsp sugar
1/4 tsp baking soda
1/4 tsp sage
6 Tbsp cold shortening
4 Tbsp cold butter
2 cups buttermilk
1 cup heavy cream
1 1/2 cups cake flour
1 Last Will and Testament

Chew on This

When making
biscuits at the
"Dinner & a Movie"
test kitchen, we
prefer using a good
Southern flour
made from soft
winter wheat.
If unavailable
in your area, try
substituting cake
flour. Lower in
protein and gluten,
it's guaranteed to
give you biscuits
"to die for."

INSIDE SCOOP

Meg Ryan and
Dennis Quaid met
while working on
the film *Innerspace*
but didn't get
together until
this movie.

Dig Your Own Gravy:

1. Brown the sausage in a large, heavy skillet over medium heat. Transfer sausage to a plate and set aside.

2. Discard all but 3 Tbsp of drippings from the pan; add the mushrooms and onion and cook until lightly browned, about 3 minutes.

3. Add the flour and cook, stirring constantly until the flour begins to brown, about 3 minutes.

4. Add the chicken stock and cream and continue cooking until thickened.

5. Add the cooked sausage and thyme and season to taste with salt, pepper and Tabasco.

Get Your Biscuits in Order:
1. Preheat oven to 475°F. Butter a muffin tin, round cake pan or pie plate.

2. Sift together the self-rising flour, sugar, baking soda, and ground sage into a large mixing bowl.

3. Cut the shortening and butter into small pieces and work into the flour mixture until the lumps are no larger than small peas.

4. Add the cream and buttermilk and stir together just until the mixture becomes cohesive. It will be too sticky to handle. Allow the mixture to stand about 5 minutes.

5. Dump the cake flour onto a clean work surface in a pile. Dust hands with flour and pinch off biscuit-sized lumps of dough.

6. Quickly roll dough through the cake flour and roll lightly between your hands to form a ball and transfer to a muffin tin or crowd together into a cake pan or pie plate.

7. Brush with cream or melted butter and bake about 30 minutes or until proud, puffy and golden. Remove from oven and brush with melted butter if desired.

8. Cheer up: Look on the bright side, death is merely nature's way of telling you to slow down a little and let someone else do the dishes. Yield: Makes enough to last the rest of your life . . .

DID YOU KNOW?
This movie was based on the 1950 film-noir classic of the same name.

Heavenly Wings

Date with an Angel
(1987)

You'll think you're in heaven when you make a date with these wings . . .

For the Dressing:
3 Tbsp yellow onion, finely chopped
1 large clove garlic, minced
2 Tbsp fresh cilantro, peeled and minced
1/2 tsp each: ground cumin, salt, and sugar
1/4 cup buttermilk
1 cup sour cream
2 tsp Worcestershire sauce
2 tsp cider vinegar
1 4-oz can Ortega™ brand diced chilies

For the Wings:
4-6 jalapeño peppers
1/2 stick butter (4 oz)
1/2 cup Louisiana-style hot pepper sauce
1 Tbsp white vinegar
1/4 tsp each: celery seed, chili powder, garlic salt,
    black pepper, and ground coriander
4 lbs chicken wings
Peanut or vegetable oil for frying
Della Reese's toll-free hot line

Chew on This

69% of Americans believe in the existence of angels. 7% believe Elvis is still alive. We presume the other 24% of the population is comprised of faithless squares.

1. Make the Dressing: Combine all dressing ingredients except chilies in a food processor or blender and blend well.

2. Transfer to a mixing bowl; stir in Ortega™ diced chilies; cover and refrigerate.

3. Prepare the Wings: Preheat the oven to 375°F. Trim and discard the wing tips, then cut in two at the joint if desired. Pat dry with paper towels.

4. Heat the oil in a fryer or large Dutch oven over medium-high heat to 375°F-400°F. Fry the wings in batches of three or four for 10 minutes per batch. Drain on paper towels.

5. Roast the jalapeños over an open flame or under the broiler until the skin blisters and blackens. Coarsely chop and transfer to a small saucepan over medium heat.

6. Add butter, hot pepper sauce, white vinegar, celery seed, chili powder, garlic salt, black pepper, and coriander; cook 5 minutes until the mixture comes to a boil.

7. Transfer wings to a large mixing bowl and toss with the jalapeño sauce. Arrange on sheet pans and bake for 20-25 minutes.

8. Grab your wings and dressing, then head outside to search the night sky for any heavenly bodies that like to do dishes.
Yield: 4 servings

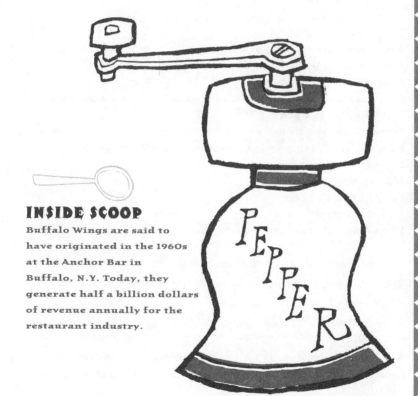

INSIDE SCOOP

Buffalo Wings are said to have originated in the 1960s at the Anchor Bar in Buffalo, N.Y. Today, they generate half a billion dollars of revenue annually for the restaurant industry.

Food for Thought

Best known as the legendary "Tad Martin" from the popular soap opera, "All My Children," Michael E. Knight originally joined the soap in 1982, but has left twice to pursue a career in the movies. Through the years, Tad has suffered from amnesia, bedded mothers and daughters and hosted his own TV talk show. At press time, he was gearing up for marriage number five and bonding with his long-lost half brother, an African-American secret agent.

Super Extra Meaty Meat Loaf

Deceived
(1991)

This classic thriller features Goldie Hawn as a wife who's been dealt the ultimate deception. But don't worry, we would never deceive you. We're TV people. You can trust us. This is the meatiest meatloaf ever. It's positively chock full of delicious, juicy, life-giving Meaty-Meat®. Would we lie to you? Of course not, we're TV people.

1 cup cashew nuts
1/2 cup walnuts
1/2 cup pine nuts
2 Tbsp butter
1 cup leeks, finely chopped
1 Tbsp garlic, peeled and finely chopped
1 cup mushrooms, chopped
1/2 ounce dried mushrooms, soaked in 1/2 cup warm water
 and finely chopped
Salt and pepper to taste
1 Tbsp each: fresh parsley, thyme and basil, chopped
1 cup cooked brown rice
1/2 cup Grape Nuts™
1 cup cottage cheese
3 eggs, beaten
1 Acme brand "fake your own death kit®"

1. Toast the nuts on a baking sheet at 350°F for 10 minutes.

2. Coarsely chop the cashews and walnuts (leave the pine nuts whole) and set aside.

3. Sauté the leeks in butter until softened, but not brown. Add the garlic and reduce the heat to medium.

4. Add the chopped mushrooms to the mushroom soaking liquid and cook over medium heat about 10 minutes. Season with salt and pepper to taste.

Chew on This

MUSHROOM TIP #27

Because mushrooms are grown in a sterile hothouse environment, there's no need to soak or rinse them heavily with water before cooking. Mushrooms will absorb the excess water and ultimately lose flavor.

5. Transfer the hot mixture to a large mixing bowl and add the herbs, toasted nuts, brown rice, Grape Nuts™, cottage cheese, eggs, and mix well.

6. Butter a 1 1/2 quart baking dish or loaf pan and fill with the mixture and bake for 60 minutes. The top should be firm and nicely brown, but not burned. (Brush with tomato sauce or ketchup for the final 20 minutes, if desired.)

7. Serve up your meatless meatloaf secure in the knowledge that even your most carnivorous guest may be deceived by its hearty goodness.

8. Deploy your Acme brand "fake your own death kit ®" proving you'll do whatever it takes to avoid doing the dishes.
Yield: Serves 600

INSIDE SCOOP

Fooled you! Her real name is Goldie Studlendgehawn.

Food for Thought

Where's the beef? Everywhere, apparently! If you think you're a vegetarian, you better think again. Less than 50 percent of an average steer ends up as a retail beef cut. The remainder ends up as (among other things) cosmetics, toothpaste, chalk, shampoo, car tires, explosives, buttons, violin strings, crayons, sporting equipment and insulin.

Bon Bons...
James Bon Bons

The dish is Bon Bons . . . James Bon Bons . . .

6 egg whites
1/8 tsp cream of tartar
1/4 tsp salt
2 tsp vanilla
1 3/4 cup sugar
1/4 cup saltine crackers, finely ground
1 cup pecans, finely ground
1/2 cup unsweetened chocolate, chopped
1/2 lb bittersweet chocolate
1/2 lb white chocolate
Cocoa powder, for dusting
Powdered sugar
1 license to spill

1. Preheat the oven to 300°F. Line 2 baking sheets with foil.

2. In a large mixing bowl (don't use plastic), combine the egg whites, cream of tartar, salt and vanilla. Beat rapidly until the whites begin to stand at soft peaks (although for Bond, soft peaks may not be possible).

3. Continue beating while adding the sugar a little at a time until the mixture reaches stiff peaks (much more Bond-like).

4. Using a rubber spatula, fold in the ground saltines, pecans and unsweetened chocolate.

5. Transfer the mixture to a pastry bag fitted with a plain tip and pipe 2 inch diamonds, about 1 inch apart, onto the lined baking sheets. (You can also just drop the batter from a teaspoon in globs.)

6. Bake for about 20 minutes. Turn off the oven and continue baking another 10 minutes until firm.

7. Melt the bittersweet and the white chocolate separately in bowls over a hot water bath.

8. Using a toothpick, dip the diamonds into your chocolate of choice and dust with powdered sugar and cocoa.

9. Employ your best Bond impersonation and explain to your waiting cadre of guests and intruders that these are not just bon bons, they're James bon bons. (Don't forget to save a few for yourself. Unlike the real thing, diamonds this tasty can't possibly last forever.)
Yield: Makes about 2 dozen James bon bons

INSIDE SCOOP

This marked Sean Connery's return to the Bond role after a one-film hiatus in which the ill-fated George Lazenby tried to fill Bond's shoes in *On Her Majesty's Secret Service*.

Bumpin' Grinders (with Smoldering Loins)

Dirty Dancing
(1987)

Go back to your playpen, baby. We'll call you when you're old enough for a bumpin' grinder.

For the Smoldering Loins:
2 pork tenderloins
1/2 cup good quality soy sauce
2 tsp canned chipotle pepper, chopped (smoked Mexican jalapeño peppers, found in most supermarkets)
1 Tbsp garlic, peeled and chopped
2 tsp oregano, crushed
3 Tbsp peanut oil
2 Tbsp brown sugar
1 life (that you had the time of)

Accessorize, People!:
2 red or yellow bell peppers, thinly sliced
1 red onion, thinly sliced
1 fennel bulb, thinly sliced
3 scallions, sliced in half
1 cup tasty black or green olives, pitted and sliced
4 freshly baked Italian or French rolls
A cold shower
1 expandable dance belt

1. Work Those Loins: Place the pork loins, soy sauce, chipotle, garlic, oregano, peanut oil, and brown sugar in a zip-lock plastic bag or non-reactive container and refrigerate at least 20 minutes and no more than 12 hours.

2. Preheat the oven to 500°F.

3. Remove the pork from the marinade and place on an oiled rack set in a shallow roasting pan. Reserve the marinade for later use.

4. Roast the tenderloins in the upper third of the oven for 15 minutes;

Chew on This

Many older cookbooks recommend cooking pork to an internal temperature of 180 degrees Fahrenheit. Because the trichinae parasite can not survive temperatures above 140 degrees, we feel that cooking pork to a temperature of 160–165 degrees will produce pork that is safe yet still tender, moist and delectable.

turn over and roast an additional 10-15 minutes. (If using an instant-read thermometer, it should read at least 150°F.) Allow your meat to rest at least 10 minutes before slicing (ouch).

5. While your meat rests, heat a dry cast-iron skillet over medium-high heat until quite hot; add the bell peppers, onion, fennel, and scallions and cook about 3 minutes until softened and fragrant; add the reserved marinade and a few tablespoons of water. Reduce the heat to medium and simmer gently for 5 minutes.

6. Split the rolls lengthwise, leaving a hinge; brush with a little olive oil and toast on a dry griddle until crisp and warm.

7. Rhythmically and suggestively pack each roll with plenty of smoldering loin; accessorize with the bell pepper sauté and olives.

8. Tell your guests that although dancing should be dirty, dishes shouldn't; and offer to teach them a new move . . . "The Dishwater Dip!"
Yield: 4 servings

"Nobody puts Baby in the corner."
—Johnny Castle

MAMBO TIP

Be the best mambo dancer on your block:
- **Don't step on any toes.**
- **Always keep your hips moving.**
- **Always, always break on two.**
—Carlton Lesmo,
"Dinner & a Movie"
choreographer

INSIDE SCOOP

Patrick Swayze's mother, Patsy, was a dancer/choreographer and he learned to dance in her studio. Although he went on to perform with several ballet companies, including the Joffrey, his first professional gig was as Prince Charming in "Disney on Parade."

Christina Applecake

Don't Tell Mom the Babysitter's Dead
(1991)

Although many of you would like to be left unsupervised with Christina Applegate, we don't recommend leaving anyone unsupervised with this moist and creamy Christina Applecake. Or you'll never get a piece for yourself . . .

Cake:
2 cups apple, peeled and grated
Juice and zest of 1 lemon
1/2 cup pineapple, freshly chopped
1/2 cup dried cranberries
1 cup pecans, chopped
1/2 cup pure maple syrup
1 cup sugar
1 tsp baking powder
1 tsp baking soda
1 tsp salt
2 tsp cinnamon
1/2 tsp each: allspice, ground cloves, ground ginger
3 eggs, beaten
1 cup vegetable oil
1 1/2 cups all-purpose flour

Topping:
8 oz cream cheese
4 oz butter, softened (1/2 stick)
4 oz crystallized ginger, chopped
A good alibi

Food for Thought

Apple of my eye: Recent scientific research states that the mere fragrance of apples can actually stop those pesky anxiety attacks in their tracks.

1. Preheat the oven to 350°F.

2. Mix the apples, lemon juice, pineapple, cranberries, pecans and maple syrup together in a mixing bowl and set aside.

3. Combine the sugar, baking powder, baking soda, salt and spices and mix together well.

4. Add the beaten eggs to the spice mixture and beat well; then slowly whisk the oil into the egg mixture to form an emulsion.

5. Alternately fold the flour and the apple mixture into the egg mixture. Mix well.

6. Transfer the batter into 2 greased and floured loaf pans and bake in the center of the oven for 45 minutes, or until a knife inserted in the center comes out clean. Cool on a wire rack.

7. Combine the cream cheese, butter and ginger in the work bowl of a food processor and process until well combined. Spread liberally over cooled cake.

8. Tell your guests you've just discovered the dishwasher's dead and, well . . . you know the rest.

Yield: Makes two 9-inch loaves

THE TRUTH IS RIGHT HERE.

As "X Files" fanatics are fond of telling us, this is David Duchovny's film debut.

INSIDE SCOOP

The star of her own hit sitcom, "Jesse," Christina Applegate is perhaps best known for playing the dumb blonde Kelly Bundy on "Married With Children" (1987–1997). She made her acting debut on the soap opera "Days of Our Lives" when she was just an infant.

Nosferatuna Melts

Dracula: Dead and Loving It
(1995)

(A wolf howls in the distance) *Leesten to thee cheeldren of thee night . . . vat muzeek they make!* Contrary to popular belief, they're not howling for blood, they're just politely asking for seconds on these tasty tuna treats.

1 lb tuna steak
10 whole black peppercorns
1 Tbsp salt
15-20 whole cloves garlic, peeled
2 green onions, thinly sliced
1/4 cup red onion, finely chopped
1-2 Tbsp Sambal chili paste
1 tsp lemon zest
1 Tbsp mayonnaise
2 Tbsp extra-virgin olive oil
8 slices sourdough bread
1 1/2 cups feta cheese, crumbled
1/4 cup cilantro, chopped
1 steel mesh turtleneck

1. In a large saucepan, bring 2 or 3 inches of water to a boil; add the peppercorns, salt and garlic; boil for 5 minutes.

2. Add the tuna steak to the boiling water, reduce heat and simmer no more than 4 minutes.

3. Remove the tuna and immediately immerse in ice water until cool.

4. Slice tuna as thinly as possible and set aside.

5. Strain the garlic from the water and chop as finely as possible.

6. Combine the tuna with the chopped garlic, green and red onion, chili paste, lemon zest, mayonnaise, olive oil and mix together well.

7. Preheat oven broiler on high.

8. Top each piece of sourdough with the tuna mixture and top with crumbled feta.

Food for Thought

How do you ID a vampire?
a) If their driver's license is more that 200 years old and
b) If no one appears in the photo.

9. Broil the Nosferatuna melts just long enough to warm the feta (2 to 3 minutes). Garnish with cilantro and serve with ice-cold beer (or body temperature Bloody Marys).

10. Once dinner is over, quickly and mysteriously retire to your coffin, leaving your dishes for Renfield. (If you don't have a Renfield, any dinner guest who eats bugs and calls you Master will do.)

Yield: 4 servings

Chew on This

Long regarded as a vampire deterrent, it has been said that garlic first sprouted in the Garden of Eden in the footprints of Lucifer. Believed to have curative powers, garlic was used by the British Army during WWI to treat both tuberculosis and infections in the field.

INSIDE SCOOP

Funnyman Mel Brooks directed this *Dracula* spoof as a companion piece to his *Young Frankenstein.*

Just the Facts, Ham

Dragnet
(1987)

Your name is chef. You carry a spatula. Your mission is to protect and serve . . . dinner. You have the right to remain in the kitchen. You have the right to an apron. If you don't have an apron, we can provide you with one. Anything you burn can and will be used against you at the dinner table.

The recipe you're about to make is true. The ingredients have been named to make them easier to cook.

1 gallon water
1 cup brown sugar
4 12-oz bottles stout beer
4 to 6-lb smoked ham, fully cooked
1/2 cup each: chopped onion, carrots and celery
1 tsp ground sage
1/2 cup Marsala or sherry
6 Tbsp honey or pure maple syrup
1 Tbsp dry mustard
3 Tbsp orange marmalade
Whole cloves
The will to serve (hot) and to protect (your reputation in
   the kitchen)

1. Preheat the oven to 375°F. Combine the water, brown sugar and two of the beers in a large pot over high heat.

2. Scrub the ham well under cold, running water and set in the water and beer. When the water comes to a simmer, reduce the heat to low and cover.

3. Simmer covered for 20 minutes, then remove the pot from the heat and allow the ham to sit in the hot cooking liquid an additional 15 minutes.

4. Place ham, fat-side up, (or cut-side down if using a half ham) on a rack in a roasting pan, toss the vegetables and sage around it and pour the second beer over the top.

5. Set the roasting pan over medium-high heat on the range top until the stout begins to boil; cover, transfer to the oven and bake for one hour.

Food for Thought

Novelist
James Ellroy
(L.A. Confidential)
credits Jack Webb's
nonfiction book
Badge Of Honor
for helping to
inspire his early
interest in crime.

6. Meanwhile, whisk together the orange marmalade, Marsala, dry mustard and maple syrup; set aside.

7. Remove ham from the oven and increase the oven temperature to 400°F.

8. Slice off the rind (if it has one) and lightly score the fat in a latticework design, a pinwheel or the shape of an LAPD badge. Stud decoratively with cloves if desired.

9. Brush the Marsala mixture over the surface of the ham and bake uncovered for 15 to 20 minutes or until nicely glazed and golden brown.

10. During the last few minutes of cooking, baste every five minutes or so, taking care not to let the glaze burn.

11. Strain and degrease the pan juices to serve alongside the ham as-is, or combine with a little cream and reduce till thickened.

12. You've finished your work, what do you see . . . just a ham? . . . Well, that's not all I see, Mister. I see the good people of this city lined up with arms akimbo waiting to try an honest piece of pork grown by thousands of proud hog farmers working hard to produce a leaner, more healthful pork product . . .
Yield: 12-16 servings

INSIDE SCOOP

"Dragnet" began as a radio show in 1949 and in 1952 it moved to television, spawning several successful runs of the series.

Chew on This

Did you know. . .a good country ham is often smoked for more than a month.

Soup on a Stick

Dumb and Dumber
(1994)

You don't have to be the sharpest tool in the shed to make a darn good soup on a stick. Just try to follow this simple recipe and look up any big words.

For the Soup:
1 lb large shrimp
4 lbs chicken backs and necks
2 fresh ginger, thinly sliced
1/2 tsp black peppercorns
2 scallions, cut into 2-inch pieces
3 cloves garlic, peeled & crushed
1/4 cup dried mushrooms (optional)
4 quarts cold water
1 tsp salt

For the Stick:
1 lb beef tenderloin, well trimmed
1 lb pork tenderloin, well trimmed
1 lb chicken breasts, skinned and boned
8 oz firm tofu
1 English cucumber, cut in 3/4-inch cubes
6 scallions, cut in 2-inch pieces

For Service:
3 Tbsp soy sauce
2 Tbsp sesame oil
1 tsp chili paste
2 tsp white vinegar
1/2 napa cabbage, sliced thin
1/2 lb baby spinach, stems removed
In case of dumb kitchen accidents: 1 phone book to look up
    the number for 911

1. Try to Make the Soup: Peel and devein the shrimp. Arrange on a platter, cover and refrigerate. Combine shrimp shells with the chicken backs, ginger, peppercorns, scallions, garlic and mushrooms in a large, heavy pot. Cover with cold water and bring to a rapid boil over

> "I love California. I practically grew up in Phoenix."
> —Dan Quayle
> Attributed to former Vice President/ Presidential candidate

Chew on This

Since hitting it big with *Dumb & Dumber*, the Farrelly Brothers went on to direct another huge success, *There's Something About Mary*. However, there's no truth to the rumor that they've also launched a new line of hair care products in easy-to-use, pump-action dispensers.

high heat. Skim the surface to remove any fat that floats to the top. Partially cover the pot, reduce heat, and cook at a low simmer for at least 1 hour, preferably 2. Strain liquid through a fine strainer into a large bowl; skim off any fat that rises to the top, salt to taste and set aside. Important: Avoid submerging head or extremities in the broth until it has cooled.

2. Try Not to Hurt Yourself: Slice the beef, pork and chicken breast across the grain as thinly as possible and arrange on a platter. (When slicing the meats, may we suggest a knife?)

3. In a small bowl, mix together the soy sauce, sesame oil, chili paste and white vinegar. In a medium bowl, toss together the napa cabbage and spinach.

4. Try to Serve Dinner: Place an electric skillet or wok in the center of the table and bring the broth to a simmer. Arrange the uncooked foods around the simmering broth and ask the dumbest person present to please come forward. (If everyone steps forward, pick the person with the cleanest hands.) Explain slowly and clearly that they have the great honor of preparing the soup for everyone and that you're genuinely sorry they won't have the time to eat.

5. Have Mr. Lucky begin preparing the skewers by alternating the tofu, cucumber, and scallions with little rolled-up slices of meat on each skewer (draw a simple diagram if necessary). Submerge the skewers in the simmering broth just long enough to cook the meat, about 2 minutes.

6. Using a fork, push the cooked meat and vegetables off the skewers and into soup bowls. Put a handful of the cabbage and spinach mixture in each bowl. Top with a ladleful of hot broth and a dollop of chili-soy sauce.
Yield: 6-8 servings

INSIDE SCOOP

When a recipe calls for very thin slices of meat or chicken, try freezing it partially for an hour or so. Slicing will be much easier.

Missing Link Sausage Nachos & Ice Age Slushies

Valley boy Pauly Shore digs up a frozen caveman in his friend's backyard. Hard to believe? Who cares! The missing link is Brendan Fraser in a loin cloth and, dude, we are like, so there.

For the Slushies:
1 cup water
2 1/2 cups sugar
3 cups fresh or frozen raspberries, cherries or other tasty and colorful fruit
1 lemon, peeled with pith removed
1/2 cup packed fresh mint leaves
4 cups crushed ice

For the Nachos:
1 lb. chorizo or hot sausage
1 8-oz can refried beans
1 8-oz can black beans
1 large bag tortilla chips
1 cup shredded sharp cheddar cheese
1 cup shredded Jack cheese
1/2 cup olives, sliced
1/2 cup pickled jalapeños, sliced
1/2 cup scallions, sliced
1 avocado, thinly sliced
1 cup of your favorite salsa
1/2 cup sour cream
1/2 bunch cilantro, chopped
1 set opposable thumbs

1. For the Slushies: Combine the sugar and water in a heavy saucepan over medium-high heat and bring to a boil.

2. Boil for 5 minutes, remove from heat, and set aside. (Unused mixture can be refrigerated and used at another time.)

MANY ARE COLD BUT FEW ARE FROZEN

As of 1998, 75 people in the U.S. were in "cryonic suspension" and almost 500 more were planning to pay the $125,000 fee to be frozen after death. Almost 25% of these cryonic patients have opted to have only their heads frozen for 1/2 the fee. A penny saved...

3. Place the lemon, fruit and mint leaves in a blender and puree at high speed until liquefied.

4. Add 4-6 tablespoons of the sugar syrup (according to desired sweetness) and the crushed ice. Puree until smooth and slushy.

5. For the Nachos: Preheat oven to 350°F. Remove casings and brown the sausage. Discard grease, add refried beans and heat until the beans soften a little.

6. In a large bowl, toss the warm sausage and bean mixture with the tortilla chips until evenly mixed.

7. Lay the coated chips out in a large baking dish and top with shredded cheese, black beans, sliced olives, pickled jalapeños and scallions.

8. Bake for 20 minutes. (First make sure that you've discovered fire.)

9. Top with avocado, salsa, sour cream and chopped cilantro.

10. Toss back your crusty mops, wease the grindage and chill.
Yield: 4 servings

INSIDE SCOOP

Nachos didn't begin as a heap of stale chips covered in pump cheese. In 1947, in Piedras Negras, Mexico at the Victory Grill, rumor has it that Chef Ignacio "Nacho" Anaya created a special snack for a group of tone-deaf, drunk American women that had just begun to sing a 5th chorus of "Besa Me Mucho." Hoping to silence them, he fried up corn tortilla wedges and topped them with melted cheese and jalapeños. The Nacho was born!
One may still dine at the birthplace of this beloved snack food at the restaurant now called El Moderno which is just across the border from Eagle Pass, Texas. But please, don't sing "Besa Me Mucho."

i Want Liver Forever, i Wanna Learn How To Fry!

LOCATION: The Streets of New York City

FADE IN: Groups of promising young cooking students wildly dancing through the streets with whisks, paring knifes, and slotted spoons. Two have leapt onto a taxi cab and are air-sautéing . . . CUT TO:

For the Marinade and Liver:
1 1/2 lbs calves' liver, sliced 1/4-inch thick,
   or as thinly as possible
2 cups cold milk
2 Tbsp finely chopped shallots
5 Tbsp extra-virgin olive oil
4 Tbsp balsamic or sherry vinegar
1 Tbsp Dijon mustard

For the Flour Mixture:
1/2 cup all-purpose flour
3/4 cup bread crumbs
1/2 tsp salt
1/4 tsp freshly ground black pepper

For the Sauce:
Pure olive oil for sautéing
3 Tbsp capers
1 Tbsp chopped shallots
1/4 cup balsamic or sherry vinegar
1 cup beef stock
3 Tbsp cold butter, cut into pieces
2 Tbsp fresh parsley, minced
1 subscription to *Daily Variety Meats*

1. The Liver Prepares: Rinse the liver well in cold water; place in a bowl and cover with cold milk while assembling the next few ingredients.

2. In a small mixing bowl, combine the shallots, olive oil, and vinegar.

Chew on This

As you can imagine, we were excited to know that *Hot Lunch* was the original title for this film.

Drain the milk well from the liver and stir in shallot marinade. Cover and refrigerate for 20 minutes.

3. Combine the flour, bread crumbs, and salt and pepper on a large plate and stir together with a fork.

4. Learn How to Fry: Heat a large frying pan over high heat with just enough oil to cover the bottom of the skillet. When the oil is very hot, dredge pieces of liver in the flour mixture and shake off the excess. Fry for no more than a minute on each side. The liver should be crisp and golden brown on the outside and a little pink in the middle. Cook in batches, transferring the cooked liver to a warm platter loosely covered with aluminum foil.

3. Sauce, "The Method": Reduce the heat under the frying pan and allow it to cool a minute before adding capers, 1 tablespoon chopped shallots, and vinegar. Boil and reduce the vinegar until syrupy; add the beef stock and reduce by half. Remove the pan from the heat and add the cold butter piece by piece, while whisking vigorously and shaking the pan. Stir in the chopped parsley.

4. Arrange the liver on serving plates and spoon some sauce over each portion.
Yield: 4 servings

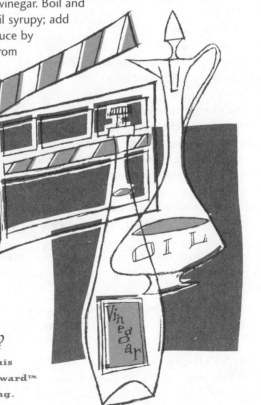

DID YOU KNOW?

The title song won this movie an Academy Award™ for Best Original Song.

Sean Penne Pasta Salad

Fast Times at Ridgemont High
(1982)

The year is 1982; kids are in the malls; the ubiquitous pasta salad is all the rage; and director Amy Heckerling is about to unleash Sean Penn on an unsuspecting public.

For the Dressing:
1/2 cup pure olive oil
1/2 tsp crushed red pepper
Juice of one lemon
1 clove garlic, minced
2 tsp fresh dill, chopped
1/4 tsp salt

For the Salad:
8 oz penne pasta
1/2 cup Nicoise olives, roughly chopped
1/4 cup cornichons, sliced
2 Tbsp capers
2 cups cherry tomatoes, quartered
1 red onion, thinly sliced
1/2 cup Romano cheese, grated
1/4 cup flat leaf parsley, roughly chopped
1 scallion, finely chopped
1 cup white beans, cooked
1 can solid white tuna, drained and flaked
1 copy Cassell's English-Surfer/Surfer-English dictionary

1. Make the Dressing: In a small mixing bowl, combine the olive oil, red pepper, lemon juice, garlic, dill and salt. Whisk together, cover and refrigerate.

2. Prepare the Pasta: Cook the pasta *al dente*, (a little less than package instructions may call for), drain, rinse well 2 or 3 times, drain again, and toss with a little olive oil.

3. Make the Salad: In a large mixing bowl, combine all salad ingredients and toss together. Whisk the dressing once more, pour over the salad and toss a few times to mix evenly.

Eating pasta is said to cause the brain to produce serotonin, a natural substance that helps bring about calmness and a sense of well-being. Next time you're feeling bogus, fill up a bowl and go party, dude.

4. Be Prepared: If you plan on eating this dish in history class, triple the recipe. That way, when the teacher says: "Did you bring enough for everyone?" you can say you did.

DAMONE'S (Robert Romanus) NEVER-FAIL 5 POINTS FOR SUCCESS WITH CHICKS

1 Never let on how much you like her.

2 Call the shots.

3 Wherever you are, *that's* the place to be.

4 Order for the both of you.

5 When making out, put on Side One of *Led Zeppelin IV*.

INSIDE SCOOP

The scene where Jeff Spicoli explains world history to Mr. Hand is supposedly the inspiration for *Bill & Ted's Excellent Adventure*.

Jennifer's Steamin' Pork Buns

We guarantee that once you bite through this steamy bun and into the succulent pork within, you'll want to cut the necks out of all your T-shirts, slip on a pair of leg warmers, and douse yourself with a bucket of cold water.

For the Buns:
3/4 cup lukewarm water
1 Tbsp active dry yeast
2 Tbsp sugar
1 Tbsp vegetable oil
1 Tbsp sesame oil
2 1/2 cups flour

For the Pork:
8 oz pork tenderloin, cut in 1/4-inch cubes
2 Tbsp soy sauce, mixed with 1 Tbsp corn starch
1 Tbsp dry sherry
2 scallions, minced
1 tsp ginger, grated
1 tsp garlic, minced
2 Tbsp Hoisin sauce
1 Tbsp sugar
1 Tbsp peanut oil
1 sweatshirt, strategically ripped

Food for Thought

Don't have a steamer? Improvise with a colander or flat strainer balanced on ramekins (small oven-proof bowls).

1. **Get Those Buns Moving:** In a small bowl, combine the warm water, yeast, sugar, and the oils. Whisk vigorously and set aside in a warm place until the yeast begins to bubble, about 10 minutes.

2. Sift 2 cups of flour into a medium mixing bowl. Gradually pour in the water and yeast mixture, stirring with a wooden spoon until the dough forms a cohesive mass.

3. Turn the dough out onto a lightly floured surface and knead for 5

minutes, adding only as much flour as needed to keep the dough from sticking.

4. Place the dough in an oiled bowl, cover with plastic wrap and set aside in a warm spot until it doubles in bulk, about 45 minutes.

5. While the dough rises, combine the pork with the soy sauce, sherry, scallion, ginger, garlic, Hoisin sauce, and sugar.

6. Heat peanut oil in a wok or heavy skillet over high heat. Add the pork mixture and stir fry 2-3 minutes. Remove from heat and cool to room temperature.

7. Remove dough to a lightly floured board and roll into a cylinder, 2 inches wide and 12 inches long. Cut into 12 pieces; flatten each piece into a 3-inch disc.

8. Place 2 Tbsp of filling in the center of each disc. Gather the dough around the filling in small pleats: twist and pinch together to seal.

9. Place each of the buns on a small sheet of foil or parchment, cover with a damp cloth and let rise 30 minutes in a warm spot.

10. Arrange in a single layer on a plate or steamer basket and steam 10-15 minutes over rapidly boiling water. Eat warm or let cool to room temperature, wrap, and refrigerate.

11. End Up With Pork Buns of Steel?: Don't fret if your buns don't puff as proudly as you'd like, they'll still be hot and tasty (and you can always call in your pork bun stand-in for the close-ups).
Yield: 12 steaming buns

INSIDE SCOOP

When this movie first came out, Jennifer Beals stunned the moviegoing public by demonstrating the complicated process involved in removing one's bra without removing one's sweatshirt.

Standing Rib Roast with Rockshire Pudding

**The Flintstones'
Christmas Carol
(1994)**

It was the best of times, it was the worst of times, it was the beginning of time, it was the Stone Age. If you've been afraid to make a standing rib roast, don't be. This recipe is easy to yabba-dabba-do.

For the Standing Rib Roast:
6 lbs prime rib (2-3 ribs, ask for "first cut")
1 Tbsp kosher salt
1 Tbsp freshly ground black pepper
2 Tbsp olive oil

For the Rockshire Pudding:
2 eggs
1 tsp salt
1 pinch nutmeg
1/4 tsp fresh thyme, minced
1 cup milk
1 cup all-purpose flour
3 Tbsp ice water
3 Tbsp fat (rendered from the roast)

For the Vegetables:
1/2 lb brussels sprouts, trimmed
1/2 lb small white onions, whole, peeled
1 lb small red potatoes, cut in half
1 stocking-full quarry rocks, freshly cracked

For the Horseradish Sauce:
4 Tbsp freshly grated horseradish mixed with 2 Tbsp white wine vinegar, or 4 Tbsp prepared horseradish
1 cup sour cream
1/4 tsp white pepper
1/2 tsp salt
1 tsp sugar

1. Prepare the Rib Roast: Adjust rack to the lower third of the oven and preheat oven to 450°F. Rinse and dry meat. In a small bowl, combine the salt, pepper, and olive oil. Rub oil into roast, and arrange fat side-up in a shallow roasting pan. Place in the preheated oven and roast for 20 minutes.

2. Reduce oven temperature to 325°F. Continue roasting for another hour, or until a meat thermometer inserted in the larger end of the roast reads about 120°F for rare, 130° for medium rare, or 140°F for medium. (If not using a meat thermometer, calculate 13-18 minutes total cooking time per pound of meat.)

3. Prepare the Veggies: Add the prepared vegetables to the roasting pan during the last 45 minutes of cooking.

4. Prepare the Rockshire Pudding: Combine the eggs, salt, nutmeg, and thyme; beat until fluffy. Alternately add the milk and flour and continue beating until smooth. Refrigerate until use.

5. Prepare the Horseradish Sauce: Squeeze excess vinegar from the grated horseradish (omit this step if using prepared horseradish). Combine with remaining ingredients and whisk until creamy. Set aside for flavors to blend.

6. Remove the roast to a platter and allow to rest at room temperature for 30 minutes before carving. This allows the roast to finish cooking evenly and gives the juices time to be reabsorbed into the meat. While the roast rests, raise the oven temperature to 400°F for the Rockshire pudding.

7. Heat rendered fat from the roasting pan in a large cast-iron skillet over medium-high heat until it begins to sizzle. Bake in the 400°F oven until puffy, crisp, and golden brown. Cool and cut into wedges. Yield: 4 servings (Save leftovers for roast-beast sandwiches.)

Gather the clan (make sure you've invited guests who have opposable thumbs), pull up your favorite rock, and give thanks for this truly prehistoric occasion.

ROAST TIP #45

Don't ask the butcher to remove the bones on your roast. They keep the roast moist and help conduct heat evenly, allowing the meat to cook in less time.

INSIDE SCOOP

Few people know that this masterful epic almost didn't make it to the big screen. According to *The Hollyrock Reporter*, it was rumored that during the filming of the movie, Fred and Wilma had creative differences. This was due to the fact that Wilma was weary of the network television grind and wanted to return to her first love, the theater, but Fred wanted to break into feature films. He felt he was being type-cast as a big Stone Age guy. At one point, Fred's confidence was so shattered he had trouble remember-ing his dialogue. "Yab ba da ba . . . Line please?" The production was halted for three days while the lawyers hammered out a compromise. Luckily for us they did. The work speaks for itself.

Kevin Bacon and Cheese Hush Puppies

This movie reminds us of a story we once heard about a small Midwestern town where all dinner parties were outlawed after a tragic fondue accident involving a rogue pair of Sunday shoes. Kids were forced to smuggle trays of hors d'oeuvres across the state line. Then, one day, a mysterious stranger rode into town. Armed with nothing but a well-seasoned, cast-iron skillet and this recipe, he freed the people with platters of finger-snappin', toe-tappin' appetizers. There was no turning back . . .

For the Batter:
1 1/2 cups cornmeal
1/2 cup all-purpose flour
1 Tbsp sugar
1 Tbsp baking powder
1/2 tsp baking soda
1/2 cup grated cheddar cheese
1 tsp salt
1 tsp ground pepper
1 egg, beaten
1/2 tsp Tabasco sauce
1 cup buttermilk
4 scallions, minced
8 slices thick bacon, cooked and crumbled into bits
1/2 cup corn
3 Tbsp cold water, if needed
Corn oil for frying
1/4 cup grated Parmesan cheese
1 empty factory with disco sound system and dance floor
1 angry and sensitive (but masculine) solo dance routine

INSIDE SCOOP

Talk about your 6 degrees of Kevin Bacon! In real life, Kevin Bacon's dancing body double (Peter Tramm) in *Footloose* was married to the dancing body double (Marine Jahan) for Jennifer Beals in *Flashdance*. There's no truth to the rumor that the couple's infant was the dance double for Ally McBeal's dancing baby.

1. Cook the bacon until crisp. Cool and crumble into little bits.

2. Stir together the following ingredients in a medium mixing bowl: cornmeal, flour, sugar, baking powder, baking soda, cheddar cheese, salt, and pepper. In a second bowl, mix together the beaten egg, Tabasco, buttermilk, scallions, bacon, and corn.

3. Heat 2 inches of oil in a heavy saucepan over medium-high heat.

4. Pour the egg mixture into the cornmeal mixture all at once and stir to make a very thick batter. (Add the cold water only if the batter seems too thick.)

5. Scoop out rounded spoonfuls of batter and drop into the hot oil. (Don't overcrowd; they need room to dance.) Fry until golden brown, about 1 minute on each side. Roll the hot hush puppies in grated Parmesan cheese and listen to the howls of delight.

Yield: 2 dozen pups

Chew on This

Try using shoehorn to remove kernels from an ear of corn. (May we suggest washing it off first?)

Food for Thought

Remember, when hush puppies are outlawed, only outlaws will have hush puppies.

The Chosen Won Ton Soup

The Golden Child
(1986)

In this 1986 comic adventure, Eddie is chosen to find a kidnapped boy destined to become the leader of someplace vaguely spiritual and not unlike Tibet. Here at "Dinner & a Movie" we believe in a more specific form of spiritual fulfillment; namely, snacks! Inspired by the curried broths of the Himalayas and Tibetan-style won tons, this is quite simply the perfect soup. Enlightenment in a bowl.

For the Won Tons:
1 1/2 cups all-purpose flour
1/2 tsp salt
1/2 tsp baking powder
1 egg, beaten
3-4 Tbsp cold water
If you prefer, pre-made
  won ton skins are available
  at most supermarkets, wimp

For the Filling:
2 Tbsp clarified butter
1 Tbsp garlic, finely chopped
2 tsp grated ginger
1 serrano pepper, finely
  chopped
1/2 small red onion, chopped
1/2 tsp curry powder
Pinch ground cloves
1 1/2 cups cooked potato
2 Tbsp cilantro, chopped
1 tsp soy sauce

For the Soup:
2 tsp vegetable oil
1 carrot, cut into matchstick-sized pieces
1 stalk celery, cut into matchstick-sized pieces
4 coin-sized pieces ginger
1/2 tsp cinnamon
1/2 cup thinly sliced portabella mushrooms
1 28-oz can peeled tomatoes, pureed
2 cups water or vegetable broth
1 tsp white vinegar
1 tsp soy sauce
3 scallions, thinly sliced
The humble ability to transcend time, space and dimension

Food for Thought

Most people assume
that all Buddhists
are vegetarian
but that's not
necessarily true.
Tibetan Buddhists,
for instance, will
eat meat, provided
the animal was
either killed by
another animal or
wandered
off a cliff.

AAAA
AAAA
AAAA
HHH
HHH
HH!

—Soup's on!

1. Make the Won Ton Skins: Sift together the flour, salt and baking powder. Make a well in the center and pour in the beaten egg. Add the water a little at a time as needed and knead until a smooth, elastic dough is formed.

2. Roll the dough out until paper-thin on a clean, dry surface, sprinkling with a little flour as needed to keep from sticking.

3. Cut first into 3-inch strips and then again to form 3-inch squares. Cover with plastic wrap or a damp cloth until ready to fill.

4. Make the Won Ton Filling: Heat clarified butter in a medium skillet over medium-high heat. Add the garlic, ginger, pepper and red onion and cook about 2 minutes.

5. Add the curry powder and cloves. Lower the heat to medium and cook another minute.

6. Scrape the mixture into a mixing bowl and combine with the cooked potato, cilantro and soy sauce. Season with salt and pepper if desired.

7. Make the Soup: Heat the vegetable oil in a large saucepan over medium-low heat. Add the carrots, celery, ginger and cinnamon and cook for 5 minutes.

8. Add the mushrooms, tomatoes and water and bring to a boil. Reduce heat to a simmer and cook 20 minutes.

9. Stuff the won tons: Using a pastry brush or the top of your finger, lightly moisten the edges of the won ton skin with beaten egg; place a teaspoon of the filling in the center, then fold the won ton in half to form a triangle. Bring the outer corners together, pinch and seal with a dab of egg wash. Allow to dry for 10-15 minutes before cooking.

10. Cook the won tons in a large pot of rapidly boiling water for 2 minutes, then place about 4 or 5 in each bowl.

11. Season the soup to taste with soy sauce and vinegar and ladle over the hot won tons. Garnish with chopped scallions.

12. Suddenly appear as if by magic before your guests balancing a steaming bowl of chosen won ton soup in each of your six hands. Don't be surprised if no one offers to help with the dishes (after all—how many people can wash, dry and stack all at the same time?).
Yield: 6 servings

INSIDE SCOOP

In this movie, the golden child is actually played by a girl, the young actress J. L. Reate.

Golden Ladyfingers

Goldfinger
(1964)

We think even James Bond would approve of this next recipe. It calls for three of his favorite ingredients: ladies, liquor, and gold.

3 large eggs, separated
1/2 cup sugar
1 tsp vanilla extract
3 Tbsp Goldschläger™ liquor (containing real gold flakes), divided
8 oz mascarpone, softened (if this Italian cream cheese is not available, use softened plain cream cheese whipped with 1 Tbsp sour cream)
24 ladyfingers, cut in half lengthwise
1 cup cold espresso or strong coffee
1 cup whipping cream
1/8 cup unsweetened cocoa
1/2 oz white chocolate
1 copy of Shirley Bassey's greatest hit . . . "Goldfingaaaah"

THINGS YOU WOULD NEVER HEAR JAMES BOND SAY

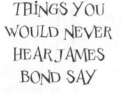

1 "Excuse me, miss, was it good for you?"

2 "No alcohol for me: I'm on antibiotics."

3 "How much do you think I should tip?"

1. Combine the egg yolks, sugar, vanilla, and 2 tablespoons of Goldschläger™ in a medium mixing bowl. Place the bowl over a saucepan of simmering water and beat until pale yellow, thick, and hot, about 10 minutes. Scrape the mixture into a large bowl, add the mascarpone, and beat until smooth. In a separate bowl, beat the egg whites until soft peaks form and fold gently into the mascarpone mixture.

2. Lay out the ladyfingers on a cooking sheet and brush both sides lightly with espresso. Set out 8 martini glasses or wine goblets. Arrange a layer of ladyfingers in each glass; top with a spoonful of the cheese mixture. Repeat with another layer of ladyfingers, followed by another spoonful of the cheese mixture. Place the glasses on a tray and freeze 30-45 minutes.

3. Whip the cream with 1 tablespoon of Goldschläger™ and spoon a little over each dessert. Dust with unsweetened cocoa and grate a little white chocolate over each before serving.
Yield: 8 servings

While you are waiting for the ladyfingers to chill, use the rest of the bottle of Goldschläger™ and a paintbrush to reenact any favorite scenes from the movie.

Young at Hearts of
Romaine Seizure Salad

What the hell are you lookin' at, wisenheimer?! Never seen a foolproof recipe for a perfect Caesar salad? Well shut your pie hole and maybe you'll learn something. In our day, people used to walk ten miles through the snow for a good Caesar…

For the Dressing:
8 anchovy filets (reserve oil)
1 egg yolk (or substitute 1 Tbsp mayonnaise)
1 1/2 tsp Dijon mustard
1 Tbsp garlic, finely chopped
1 tsp freshly ground black pepper
2 Tbsp fresh lemon juice
1 tsp red wine vinegar
1 tsp Worcestershire sauce
1 cup good Parmesan cheese,
   freshly grated
3/4 cup pure olive oil
   (not extra-virgin)
2 Tbsp ice water

For the Croutons:
2 Tbsp pure olive oil
2 Tbsp reserved anchovy oil
1 Tbsp garlic, finely chopped
1 tsp fresh thyme, chopped
1 baguette, cut into 1/4-inch cubes
Salt and pepper to taste

For the Salad:
6 hearts of Romaine, washed and chilled
1 bone to pick
1 grudge held, with gusto

Food for Thought

Forget the Viagra, the anchovies in a traditional Caesar salad are believed to have aphrodisiacal properties. (FYI…so do pomegranates, watercress, dates, chocolate, pickles, asparagus and of course, snails. That would explain those yearnings while gardening.)

1. Dressing, I'm supposed to make dressing? In a medium mixing bowl, mash half of the anchovy filets. Add the egg yolks, mustard, garlic, black pepper, lemon juice, vinegar, Worcestershire and 1/2 cup of the grated Parmesan. Whisk all ingredients together, making sure to complain audibly if the movement causes any pain.

2. All this exercise can't be good. Add the olive oil in a slow steady stream, while whisking constantly. (If you haven't alienated everyone within earshot, it's a good idea to ask someone to help by trickling in the oil a little at a time while you whisk.) Keep whisking until all the oil has been emulsified and the dressing (and most likely your whisking arm) is quite stiff. If the dressing gets a little too thick, whisk in a couple of tablespoons of ice water.

3. What's with the fancy toast on my salad? Combine the anchovy oil, olive oil, garlic, thyme, salt and pepper in a large skillet and place over medium heat. Add the croutons and toss to coat with the oil. Continue cooking until the croutons begin to turn golden brown, stirring constantly.

4. My heart, it's my heart! Tear the hearts of Romaine into bite-sized pieces or larger, depending on the fit of your dentures.

5. Sorry, false alarm...(not that you care). Toss the hearts with a ladle full of the dressing. Pile onto chilled plates and top with warm croutons, anchovies, and grated Parmesan. (Feel free to serve with any fresh grilled catch from recent ice-fishing excursions or "no spring chicken" breast.)

6. Goodness, what a lovely evening this has been! Muster all available acting prowess and make the transformation into "chipper and adorable curmudgeon" just long enough to recruit plenty of help with the dishes. Then kick everybody out and watch the lottery results!
Yield: 4-6 servings

WARNING: This is our version of the classic Caesar which uses raw eggs in the dressing. This generally poses no problem for healthy adults. However, when serving to anyone very old (e.g., Lemmon or Matthau), very young or with health problems, we suggest substituting one tablespoon of mayonnaise for each egg yolk.

Chew on This

We've seen the future and it's really grumpy. Today 1 in 8 Americans is over 65 but, by the year 2030, that number will be 1 in 4.

INSIDE SCOOP

Including *Grumpy Old Men*, Jack Lemmon and Walter Matthau have starred in 12 movies together. Their collaboration started in 1966 with *The Fortune Cookie*. Lemmon also directed Matthau in *Kotch*.

Bigfoot Longs

During our search for the elusive "healthful-yet-tasty hot dog," there were times when we felt we had a better chance of finding Sasquatch at a swap meet. It seems we underestimated ourselves. This very low-fat, all-chicken foot long is loaded with flavor, while the only Yeti sightings we've witnessed so far have been in this 1987 comedy starring John Lithgow. (Although a friend of ours thought she saw a chupacabra at the car wash once.)

3/4 lb chicken thigh meat, skinned and boned
3/4 lb chicken breast meat, skinned and boned
1 tsp soy sauce
1 tsp garlic, minced
1 egg white
1/2 tsp onion powder
2 tsp paprika
1 1/2 tsp salt
1/4 tsp celery seed
1/4 tsp ground sage
1/2 tsp white pepper
1 1/2 tsp sugar
1 cup ice cubes
1 very large flea collar

Food for Thought

The hot dog was given its current name in 1901. Until that time, the product had been sold under the name "red-hot dachshund sausages." (Perhaps someone had trouble spelling dachshund.)

1. Cut the chicken in 1/2-inch pieces and place in a medium mixing bowl. Stir in the soy sauce, garlic and egg white. In a small bowl, combine the onion powder, paprika, salt, celery seed, sage, white pepper, and sugar. Pour the spice mixture over the chicken and mix in well. Place the bowl in the freezer and chill for 30 minutes.

2. Put the ice cubes in the bowl of a food processor fitted with a metal cutting blade. Process for 30 seconds until well pulverized; scrape the ice into a bowl and set aside. Add the chicken to the processor bowl and grind in 2 15-second pulses, scraping the sides of the bowl with a rubber spatula between pulses. Add the crushed ice and grind for a final 20 seconds.

3. Transfer the ground chicken to a pastry bag with a 3/4-inch opening. Oil a 15-inch length of aluminum foil and pipe out 6 nice bigfoot longs side by side. Bring 1 inch of water to a boil in a large skillet or saucepan; carefully transfer the foil and the foot longs into the pan. Cover and reduce the heat to medium. Steam for 8-10 minutes. Remove the dogs and either serve hot from the pan with garnishes of choice or plunge in ice water to cool quickly before wrapping and refrigerating.
Yield: 6 bigfoot longs

INSIDE SCOOP

John Lithgow has been nominated for an Academy Award™ for Best Supporting Actor twice—for *The World According to Garp* and *Terms of Endearment*. He has also won two Emmy® Awards for his role as the alien commander on the hit sitcom "Third Rock from the Sun."

WARNING

When serving your foot longs, beware of the oft sighted North American Drop-In Dinner Guest®, a slow-moving, bloated creature spotted loping through areas where sumptuous meals have been prepared. This behemoth shouldn't be confused with the elusive North American Dishdoin' Dinner Guest®, the only apparition with fewer reported sightings than Bigfoot.

Shrunken Shanks with Pygmy Veggies in Red Wine Reduction

This is proof positive that shrinking is not always a bad thing. It inspired this recipe (which is big on taste) and made Rick Moranis realize happiness was right there at home in his bowl of cereal.

4 lamb shanks
4 cloves garlic, each cut in 6 slivers
2 tsp grated lemon zest
2 tsp kosher salt
2 tsp freshly ground black pepper
1/2 tsp sugar
1/2 cup lemon juice
4 Tbsp pure olive oil
3 Tbsp flour
1/2 cup yellow onion, coarsely chopped
1/2 cup celery, coarsely chopped
1/2 cup carrot, coarsely chopped
1 Tbsp tomato paste
1 cup pinot noir (or other tasty medium-bodied red wine)
1/2 cup tomato, peeled and chopped
1 bay leaf
1/4 bunch parsley sprigs, tied together with string
1 lb assorted baby vegetables (red potatoes, carrots, zucchini, yellow squash, etc.)
1 magnifying glass

INSIDE SCOOP

A large proportion of the lamb imported to the U.S. is from New Zealand, where sheep outnumber people 20 to 1. So why are they still so nervous?

1. Rinse shanks in cold water and trim excess fat. Using a sharp paring knife, cut six slits in the meatiest parts of each shank, inserting a garlic sliver in each slit as you go.

2. Mix together lemon zest, salt, pepper, sugar, 1 tablespoon of the olive oil, and 1/4 cup of the lemon juice. Rub this mixture well into meat. Cover and refrigerate for 20 minutes, while preparing and assembling the remaining ingredients.

3. Heat the remaining olive oil in a large, thick-bottomed pot over medium-high heat. Remove the lamb shanks from the marinade and blot dry with a paper towel; dust with flour and sear on all sides for about 5 minutes, until nicely browned. Transfer the browned shanks to a plate and set aside. Pour off all but 2 tablespoons of the fat and add the onion, celery, carrot, and tomato paste. Sauté this mixture for 2-3 minutes and then add the remaining lemon juice, wine, tomato, bay leaf, and parsley.

4. Return the meat to the pot, along with any juices on the plate. Bring to a simmer; reduce heat to low and cook covered for at least 2 hours, until meat is very tender and succulent.

5. Add the baby vegetables during the last 30 minutes of cooking. Remove the meat and vegetables to a warm platter, cover, and keep warm.

6. Spoon and discard any fat that floats to the surface, bring to a boil and reduce to a gravylike consistency. Season to taste with salt and pepper.

7. Ladle the red wine reduction over the pygmy veggies and shrunken shanks; eat rapidly.

Remember, there are no small meals, only small cooks.

Yield: 4 servings.

Food for Thought

Many of the "baby" vegetables available today are actually full-grown, miniature hybrids.

Chew on This

The "shrinking" genre is ever-expanding. Besides the two sequels to this film — *Honey, I Shrunk the Audience* and *Honey, We Shrunk Ourselves* — check out these classics:

- *The Fantastic Voyage* (1966)
- *The Incredible Shrinking Man* (1957)
- *The Incredible Shrinking Woman* (1981)
- *Innerspace* (1987)

Peter Pancakes with Lost Boysenberry Syrup

Hook
(1991)

Here's a happy thought . . . you can never be too old to enjoy pancakes and syrup for dinner!

For the Syrup:
4 cups or 1 lb fresh or frozen boysenberries
2 cinnamon sticks
1 cup water
1/2 cup light brown sugar
Pinch salt
1 cup light corn syrup
2 tsp vanilla

For the Pancakes:
2 cups all purpose flour
3/4 tsp salt
1 1/2 Tbsp sugar
1 tsp baking powder
1/2 tsp baking soda
1 1/2 cups buttermilk
3/4 cup whole milk
2 eggs, at room temperature
1/3 cup butter, melted
1/2 cup pecans
Pixie dust, to taste

DiD YOU KNOW?
Keep your eyes open and you'll see Gwyneth Paltrow making her screen debut as the young Wendy.

Food for Thought
Ladies, do you know men who exhibit signs of irresponsibility, narcissism and chauvinism? Steer clear! They may be suffering from the highly contagious and incurable "Peter Pan Syndrome" as identified in the 1983 book of the same name. When asked to comment, a spokesman for the CDC (Center for Disease Control) offered the following suggestion: "Grow up!"

1. **Make the Syrup:** Combine berries, cinnamon, water, brown sugar and salt in a saucepan. Bring to a boil, reduce heat and simmer 30 minutes.

2. Remove cinnamon and add corn syrup and vanilla. Strain if desired and keep warm until use.

3. **Make the Batter:** Toast chopped pecans in a dry skillet over medium heat for 3 or 4 minutes, stirring and tossing occasionally. Set aside.

4. Sift together the flour, salt, sugar, baking powder and baking soda into a large mixing bowl.

5. Separate the eggs.

6. In a second bowl, combine and whisk together the egg yolks and melted butter.

7. Add the milk and buttermilk to the egg yolk mixture and mix well.

8. Add the wet mixture to the dry and stir together, then fold in the pecans.

9. Whip the egg whites to soft peaks and gently fold into the batter.

10. Heat a griddle over medium-high heat until quite hot and brush lightly with vegetable oil.

11. Pour batter onto the hot griddle 3 to 4 tablespoons at a time and cook until the surface begins to bubble and volcano, about 2 minutes.

12. Flip the cakes and cook another minute and eat promptly.

13. After eating your fair share of these lofty cakes, sing a round of "I Don't Want to Grow Up"; take a nap and leave the dishes for the grownups.
Yield: 4 servings

Chew on This

Because Julia Roberts' Tinkerbell was always barefoot and often in the air, Roberts had an assistant whose "sole" responsibility was cleaning her feet.

INSIDE SCOOP

Hats off to the wily horticulturist, Rudolph Boysen, who in 1923 had enough chutzpah, moxie and vision to cross a blackberry, raspberry and loganberry to make a Boysenberry.

Man Eating Shark...and Loving It

Just when you thought it was safe to go back in the kitchen . . .

1 1/2-2 lbs shark steak or filet
2 Tbsp garlic, chopped
5 Tbsp olive oil
1 tsp chili flakes
1 tsp ground cumin
1 tsp oregano
Flour, for dusting
1 yellow onion, sliced
1/2 cup white wine
2 Tbsp capers
1/4 cup olives
3 cups tomatoes, chopped (or 1 28-oz can chopped Italian
   tomatoes)
1 12-oz bottle clam juice
2 bunches chard, washed and cut into 2-inch strips
Salt and pepper to taste
1 copy "Mack the Knife"

1. In a large mixing bowl, combine and stir together the garlic,
3 tablespoons of the olive oil, chili flakes, cumin and oregano.

2. Cut the shark into 2-inch chunks and toss with the garlic and olive
oil mixture. Set aside.

3. Heat a large skillet over medium-high heat until quite hot. Add the
remaining olive oil and swirl the pan to coat the bottom evenly.

4. Dust the shark with a small amount of flour, season with salt and
pepper and quickly sear the shark in batches until lightly browned, but
not fully cooked through.

5. Transfer the browned fish to a warm platter.

6. Reduce the heat under the skillet to medium, add the sliced onions
and sauté about 5 minutes.

INSIDE SCOOP

Steven Spielberg, who directed Jaws when he was just 26, kept the audience in suspense for an hour and twenty minutes before revealing the monster shark. With this long lead-in, he envisioned viewers would imagine a shark far worse than he could possibly create. He did his best to imbue it with a killer instinct by nicknaming it "Bruce" after his lawyer.

7. When the onion becomes translucent, add the white wine. Using a wooden spoon, scrape the bottom of the pan to loosen any tasty brown bits stuck to the surface.

8. Add the capers, olives and tomatoes and sauté a moment before adding the clam juice. Reducing the heat to low, simmer uncovered for 15 minutes.

9. Stir in the chard, cover and cook for 5 minutes.

10. Return the browned shark to the skillet and cook no more than 5 minutes, until just heated through.

11. Season to taste with salt and pepper, ladle into bowls and serve with chunks of hot garlic bread.

12. Tip: No need to worry about cleanup! Cooked properly, this dish should start a feeding frenzy that won't stop until your guests have frantically devoured everything in front of them: dishes, silverware, placemats, napkins . . .
Yield: 4 servings

Chew on This

When buying fresh shark, don't be afraid to ask the clerk for a look and a quick sniff (of the shark, that is). The meat should be firm and pink. If you detect any odor of ammonia, reject it and ask to see either the swordfish or the manager.

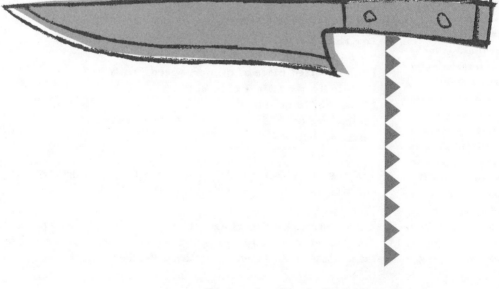

Big Jerked Chicken

The Jerk
(1979)

Although this chicken was raised by a family of poor blackbirds, it managed to pull itself up out of poverty and find its way right into your oven.

For the Jerk Seasoning:
1/3 cup cider vinegar
1 Tbsp molasses
1 Tbsp soy sauce
1 Tbsp Worcestershire sauce
Juice and zest of 1 lime
1 tsp light brown sugar
4 Tbsp butter, softened
4 scallions, chopped
3 cloves garlic, peeled
1/4 tsp black pepper
1 tsp salt
2 tsp ground cinnamon
2 tsp ground allspice
1 Tbsp fresh ginger, peeled and thinly sliced
1 habañero pepper (a.k.a. Scotch Bonnet),
  or 2-3 jalapeños, seeded

For the Chicken:
1 4-5 lb chicken
1 thumb-sized piece of ginger, sliced thinly
1 whole head garlic, cut in half
1 lime, cut in quarters
1 habañero or jalepeño pepper, halved lengthwise
1 pair opti-grabs

1. Prepare the Jerk: Measure out and combine all jerk seasoning ingredients in the work bowl of a food processor or blender. Mix until smooth.

2. Prepare the Chicken: Adjust oven rack to the center of the oven and preheat to 450°F. Rinse and dry the chicken; massage 1/2 of the jerk seasoning all over the chicken, under the breast skin, and inside

Food for Thought

Steve Martin got his start by selling 25-cent guidebooks and entertaining at Disneyland. In addition to his acting career, Martin is also a successful play-wright ("Picasso at the Lapin Agile"), author (*Pure Drivel*) and frequent contribu-tor to *The New Yorker* magazine.

the cavity. Place the ginger, garlic, lime, and habañero inside the cavity and close by tying the ends of the drumsticks together loosely.

3. Set the chicken with the breast-side down on an oiled rack in a roasting pan. Roast uncovered for 30 minutes, brushing with pan juices and jerk seasoning every 10 minutes or so. If the pan juices sizzle too loudly or begin to smoke, add 1/2 cup of water to the pan.

4. Flip the chicken breast-side up and reduce the oven temperature to 350°F. Continue roasting an additional hour, basting frequently. The chicken is done when the skin is crisp and brown and the drumsticks feel loose in their sockets. A meat thermometer inserted into the thick part of the thigh nearest the body should register 165°-175°F. Transfer chicken to a platter or carving board and let rest for 15-20 minutes before serving.

5. While the chicken rests, transfer the pan juices to a small saucepan and skim off the fat. Remove the garlic and habañero from the cavity, chop finely, and combine with the pan juices. Heat to a simmer and serve alongside the chicken.

Yield: 4 servings

INSIDE SCOOP

The practice of breaking the wishbone to see who gets the larger half dates back more than 2,000 years. It is most likely the origin of "a lucky break."

Chew on This

Believed to have come from the Spanish word *charqui* which referred to barbecued meat and later evolved into *jerky*, "jerk" dishes can be traced back to the early 17th century when Jamaican natives—in order to avoid capture by British slave traders—hid in the mountains and cooked meals beneath the earth. In doing so, they also happened to create one of the tastiest dishes ever.

New Age Baloney

L.A. Story
(1991)

Do you remember where you were when you first heard of balsamic vinegar? Probably somewhere deep in the '80s, with a mouth full of something fat-free, sugar-free and meat-free—anything but free when the check arrived. In homage to the beginnings of L.A. spa cuisine, we decided to make the only kind of baloney any self-respecting food phobic could eat . . . fish mousse.

For the New Age Baloney:
1/2 lb fresh scallops
1/4 lb red snapper
1/4 lb smoked salmon
1/2 Tbsp salt
1 tsp paprika
Pinch white pepper
Pinch nutmeg
3 egg whites
1/3 cup crushed ice
1/4 cup heavy cream

For the Dressing and Salad:
2 Tbsp raspberry vinegar
1/2 cup walnut oil
1 bell pepper, roasted, peeled and diced
1/2 cup toasted pistachios, chopped
Salt and pepper, to taste
4-5 cups unpronounceable and conspicuously expensive free range baby field greens (or just a couple of heads of lettuce)
1 earthquake survival kit

Food for Thought

Steve Martin, Coffee Prophet? When this movie was released who didn't chortle with superior disdain at the infamous coffee scene? What kind of nudnik would order a half-caf, grande, double, non-fat, soy latte? Nowadays, apparently everyone in America. All hail the Starbucks™ nation! Resistance is futile! You will be assimilated!

1. Set a large pot of water on to boil.

2. Cut scallops, snapper and salmon into small pieces and toss with the seasonings and egg whites.

3. Place in the freezer and chill for 20 minutes until very cold, but not frozen.

4. Transfer cold fish to work bowl of food processor and pulse 3 or 4 times until finely chopped.

5. Add the crushed ice and pulse 5 or 6 more times until thick and emulsified.

6. Process another 45 seconds while slowly adding the cream.

7. Spread the mixture out onto a sheet of plastic wrap, and roll tightly to resemble a large sausage. Remove from plastic, wrap tightly a second time, this time in foil, twisting the ends to seal.

8. Place in the boiling water, reduce the heat to a low simmer and poach 15-20 minutes until cooked through.

9. Transfer to a large bowl of ice water to cool.

10. Combine dressing ingredients and whisk together.

11. Slice new age baloney thinly and serve over the bed of free range baby field greens. Drizzle with raspberry-pistachio dressing.

12. Completely ignore meal and begin obsessing about recent weight gain while conspicuously wielding impossibly teeny cell phone to confirm tanning appointment.
Yield: 4 servings

Chew on This

Los Angeles isn't ALL smog, traffic jams and empty-headed hardbodies. What's not to like about a city with:

- **an average temperature of 64 degrees**
- **329 yearly days of sunshine**
- **300 museums**
- **63,000 acres of parkland (including famous Griffith Park, the largest city park in the U.S.)**
- **over 500 colonic donut shops**

Bite Your Tongue Tacos

**Look Who's
Talking Too**
(1990)

If you think this is gross, wait'll you see what we're making for *Alive*.
We call it . . . Bob.

For the Tongue:
1 lb beef tongue
1 head garlic, cut in half
2 white onions, peeled and quartered
2 carrots, coarsely chopped
2 stalks celery
Tbsp salt
3 bay leaves
5 black peppercorns
Cold water to cover
4 Tbsp peanut oil

For the Salsa:
1/2 pound tomatillos
1/2 pound tomatoes
4 cloves garlic, peeled
2 jalapeño peppers
1/2 cup cilantro, chopped
1/4 tsp salt

For Service:
1 dozen corn tortillas
Plenty of garnishes, i.e., limes, chopped cabbage, tomatoes,
   onion, cilantro, sour cream, etc.
1 box of tongue depressors

Food for Thought

What is it about
Americans that
prevents us from
enjoying foods that
honestly look like
what they are?
While the world
around us happily
asks for seconds of
this tasty organ,
many folks here
consciously avert
their eyes from it
when at the butcher.
(Usually whilst on
the way to the hot
dogs, which are well
known to be chock
full o' tongue and
look like another
organ all together.)

1. Prepare the Tongue: Scrub the tongue under running water
and place in a large pot. If the tongue is much more than 2 pounds, cut
in half lengthwise.

2. Add the garlic, onion, carrots, celery, salt, bay leaves and
peppercorns. Cover with water and set over high heat.

3. When the water comes to a boil, reduce the heat, half cover and
simmer for 45 minutes.

4. While the Tongue Simmers, Make the Salsa: Heat a dry cast-iron griddle or skillet over medium-high heat. Place the tomatillos, tomatoes, garlic and jalapeños on the griddle and pan roast for about 10 minutes, until their skins began to blister.

5. Transfer the roasted ingredients to a blender or food processor along with the salt and half of the cilantro. Puree for about 30 seconds, transfer to a bowl and stir in the remaining cilantro.

6. Remove the tongue from the pot and rinse with cold water to cool before slicing in half lengthwise.

7. Peel and discard the skin, return the trimmed meat to the simmering pot and continue cooking for 45 minutes.

8. Heat the peanut oil in a heavy skillet over medium heat. Retrieve the onions and garlic from the stock and add to the hot oil (you should be able to squeeze the garlic right from its skin into the oil); cook for 5 minutes, stirring often.

9. Remove the tongue from the stock, chop into very small pieces and add to the hot skillet along with the garlic and onion. Add a cup of the cooking liquid and cook down until the stock has evaporated, about 30 minutes. At this point, the tongue should be rich, tender and flavorful.

10. Keep warm over a low heat while heating tortillas and arranging the garnishes artfully around the table, then eat with gusto.

11. Once dinner is over, strut around the dining room like a proud parent, making speeches and passing out cigars. If anyone mentions the dishes, bite your tongue.
Yield: 6 servings

Chew on This

One of the crew members on this movie is listed as "Sperm Wrangler."

OUT OF THE MOUTHS OF BABES
The voice of Mickey is Bruce Willis, the voice of baby Julie is Roseanne and the voice of Mr. Toilet Man is Mel Brooks.

Miraculously Cured Salmon
(with a Rapidly Disappearing Rain Forest Salad)

Medicine Man
(1992)

Open wide and say mmmm . . . Sean Connery plays a hard-drinking rogue doctor searching for an Amazon miracle cure in *Medicine Man*. You won't have to search any further for the cure to hunger. This delicately smoked salmon is delicious, and making it doesn't hurt a bit. If you doubt our diagnosis, get a second opinion.

For the Salmon:
1/4 cup kosher salt
1/4 cup brown sugar
2 tsp ground coriander
1 tsp cracked black pepper
Zest and juice of 1 orange
4 8-oz salmon filets
1/3 cup each: hickory chips,
    raw brown rice and brown sugar
1 Tbsp loose tea

For the Sauce:
2 firm, ripe tomatoes, diced
2 cloves garlic, finely chopped
2 jalapeño chilies, finely chopped
2 Tbsp coconut milk
Juice of 2 limes
2 Tbsp dende oil (use peanut oil
    if unavailable)
1/4 tsp salt

For the Salad:
1 can hearts of palm, thinly sliced
1/2 cup cilantro, coarsely chopped
1/2 cup parsley, coarsely chopped
1 onion, thinly sliced
1 quart Ben and Jerry's "Rain Forest Crunch"™

Chew on This

Curing food, whether by smoke, salt or acid, is one of the oldest and tastiest forms of food preservation. Speaking of tasty preservation, Sean Connery was born 69 years ago, in Scotland.

Food for Thought

RAIN FOREST-
SAVING
KITCHEN TIP
#237

Don't stand in front of the refrigerator with the door open for more than 20 minutes.

1. Combine the salt, sugar, coriander, black pepper, orange zest and juice in a small mixing bowl.

2. Rub the salt mixture evenly over both sides of the salmon filets, cover and let refrigerate 30 minutes.

3. Meanwhile, place the wood chips in a small bowl and cover with hot water.

4. Make the Sauce: Combine all sauce ingredients in a small saucepan; heat and keep warm over a very low heat.

5. Line with aluminum foil a large, heavy pot that has a tight-fitting lid.

6. Place the soaked wood chips, brown rice, brown sugar and tea in the pot, lightly oil a wire rack and set it inside the pot, over the chips.

7. Scrape off all excess salt mixture from the salmon and arrange the filets on the oiled rack.

8. Cover the pot tightly and place over a medium heat.

9. When the pot just begins to smoke, reduce the heat to low and continue smoking another 15-20 minutes, until firm to the touch.

10. Toss together the hearts of palm, cilantro, parsley and onion.

11. Serve the salmon warm over the palm heart salad and spoon the warm dressing over each filet.

Yield: 4 servings

INSIDE SCOOP

If more people ate salmon instead of beef, the rain forest wouldn't be in danger. A significant percentage of rain forest deforestation is for beef production.

Fall-Apart Pot Roast

The Money Pit

(1986)

Unlike the dream house-turned-nightmare in this 1986 Steven Spielberg production, our pot roast is designed and constructed to fall apart. Deconstruction can be delicious!

5 lbs boneless chuck roast
1/4 cup brandy
2-3 tsp kosher salt
2 tsp freshly ground black pepper
1 tsp paprika
2 tsp garlic powder
1/2 tsp crushed thyme
2 1/2 Tbsp all-purpose flour
3 Tbsp olive oil
1 cup onions, coarsely chopped
1 cup carrots, coarsely chopped
1 cup celery, coarsely chopped
2 cups leeks, coarsely chopped
6 cloves garlic, sliced thinly
2 cups tomatoes, coarsely chopped
2 cups dry red wine
2 cups beef stock
6 parsley sprigs
1 bay leaf
3 whole cloves
4 sprigs fresh thyme
8 whole black peppercorns
10-12 small new potatoes, cut in half
1 hardhat
1 large second mortgage

Chew on This

Typically, cuts of meat used in pot roast are high in collagen, a tough connective protein that dissolves and turns to gelatin when subjected to long periods of moist heat.

Food for Thought

For a classic movie with the same theme as *The Money Pit*, check out *Mr. Blandings Builds His Dream House* starring Cary Grant and Myrna Loy.

1. Rinse roast with cold water and pat dry with paper towels. Place in a large bowl and rub well with the brandy.

2. Using a series of half-hitches, tie the roast firmly with butcher's twine. If knots make you nuts, ask the butcher for a meat wrap. They're usually free.

3. Mix together the salt, pepper, paprika, garlic powder, thyme, and flour. Rub the mixture into roast.

4. Heat the olive oil in a large Dutch oven or heavy pot over medium-high heat until almost smoking. Place roast in the hot oil and brown well on each side, about 12-15 minutes total. Transfer the roast to a plate.

5. Add the chopped vegetables, garlic, and tomatoes and sauté 5-10 minutes. Add the red wine and use a wooden spoon to scrape loose any tasty browned bits which stick to the pan.

6. Cook the red wine down by half; add the parsley, bay leaf, fresh thyme, and peppercorns. Return the meat to the pot.

7. Bring to a very low simmer. Cover tightly and cook either over a low heat or in an oven preheated to 200°F for 4-5 hours, turning the meat every half hour.

8. Add the potatoes 1 hour before serving. Important: Never allow the roast to come to a full boil. Boiling will dry out the meat.

9. Remove the meat and potatoes to a warm platter and cover. Spoon off any fat that floats to the surface of the pot juices. Transfer half of the remaining vegetables to a blender and blend well; return the blended vegetables to the pot and cook down a few minutes over high heat until thickened. Ladle gravy over meat and serve at once.

10. Pretend you're a general contractor! Tell your guests dinner will be served at 6 P.M. sharp and that you would like a five-dollar donation toward the groceries. Then don't serve dinner until midnight and charge them each forty dollars plus labor!

Yield: 6 servings

This Side-Upside-Down Cake

Moving
(1988)

Psychologists tell us that moving is one of the most stressful events a person can experience. Other stressful events include: Christmas, pregnancy, jail time and outstanding achievement. If you're looking for an outstanding achievement that's not a bit stressful, try this upside down cake. Its comforting richness makes it a great dessert for Christmas revelers, pregnant women or your favorite ex-con.

For the Topping:
1/2 cup butter
1/4 cup sugar
1/2 cup brown sugar
1/4 tsp ground cinnamon
About four cups of your favorite fruit sliced thinly: papaya, apricot, peach, pear, mango, cranberries, figs or any combination thereof. (If feeling adventurous, one might even try . . . pineapple!)

For the Sponge Cake:
2 cups flour
2 tsp baking powder
1/2 tsp salt
1 1/2 sticks butter, softened
1 cup granulated sugar
Grated zest of 1 lemon
2 tsp vanilla extract
4 eggs
1 cup milk
1 change of address form

1. Preheat oven to 350°F. Arrange rack in the center of the oven.

2. Prepare the topping: Melt the butter in a 9-10-inch cast-iron skillet over medium heat.

3. Add the sugar and brown sugar and cook until dissolved, stirring constantly. Stir in the cinnamon and remove from heat.

Chew on This

Although we think of pineapples as an Hawaiian treat, they are deliciously indigenous to the Americas.

4. Arrange all but 1 cup of the fruit artfully into the hot syrup in a single layer and set aside.

5. Prepare the sponge cake: Sift together the flour, baking powder and salt into a small bowl or on a piece of wax paper and set aside.

6. In the work bowl of an electric mixer, cream together the sugar, butter and lemon zest until fluffy.

7. Beat in the vanilla and then the eggs, one at a time.

8. Add the flour mixture in 3 batches, alternating with the milk, beating after each addition until the batter is well blended.

9. Chop the remaining fruit into small chunks and add to the batter.

10. Scrape the batter over the fruit into the skillet and smooth out the top.

11. Bake for 45-60 minutes, until the top is golden and springy. The juices should be bubbling around the sides of the pan.

12. Allow the cake to cool 5 minutes before running a knife around the edges and inverting onto a serving platter. Serve warm with whipped cream.

13. Eat quickly before the welcome wagon smells something yummy and decides to make an appearance.
Yield: One 9-10 inch cake

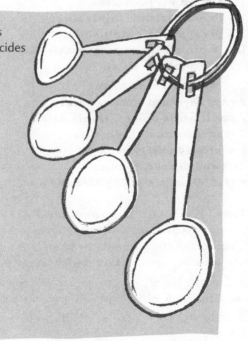

INSIDE SCOOP

Food for Thought

One of the primary ingredients of a classic upside down cake, the pineapple is also a symbol of welcome and hospitality. The Carib Indians of the West Indies hang pineapples over their hut entrances as a symbol that food and drink can be found there. At "Dinner & a Movie" we've taken the tradition a step further, choosing to hang an upside down cake above our door. Of course we hang ours right-side up.

Hollywood (Hulk) Hoagies

Mr. Nanny
(1993)

Chew on This

Hollywood
Hulk Hogan was
"discovered" while
playing bass in a
Florida nightclub in
the early '70s. His
earlier stage names
included "Sterling
Golden" and "Terry
Bolder." His first
national exposure
came in 1982, when
he appeared in
Rocky III as
the wrestler
"Thunderlips."

And now, a message from Hollywood Hulk Hogan: Get ready to rumble! You better listen up, brother (or sister) 'cause tonight you're my square meal. First, I'm gonna break your bread. Next, I'm gonna slice your salami. Then, I'm gonna pulverize your provolone. After that, I'm gonna kick your cappicola all over the ring. And just when you think you can't take anymore, I'll chew you up and not spit you out.

You're my dinner, man, 4 life.

In This Corner:
4 fresh Italian rolls
1/3 cup good olive oil
2 Tbsp red wine vinegar
1 tsp fresh oregano, chopped
1/2 tsp red pepper flakes
1/4 lb hard salami, thinly sliced
1/4 lb cappicola, thinly sliced
1/4 lb prosciutto, superhumanly thinly sliced
1/2 lb provolone, sliced

. . . And in This Corner:
2 cups shredded iceberg lettuce
2 small white onions, thinly sliced
2 ripe tomatoes, thinly sliced
4-6 pickled cherry peppers, sliced
Salt and pepper, to taste
A size 50 neck, size 22 shoes and a teeny-tiny tea set

1. Perform the Dreaded (and recently outlawed) Hinge-Hold: Body slam the rolls onto a cutting board and slice horizontally to form a painful hinge on each roll. (If you're not familiar with wrestling terms, just cut the rolls in half.)

2. Combine the oil, vinegar, oregano and pepper flakes and flagrantly brush the inside of each roll until someone pulls you off.

3. Dog Pile!: Pile the meat and cheese onto the bottom half of the rolls.

4. Top with lettuce, tomato slices, sliced onion and sliced pickled cherry peppers.

5. Drizzle a little more dressing over each sandwich and season with salt and black pepper.

6. Give 'Em a Little Taste of Your Thunder: Close up the Hoagies and serve without mercy.

7. Don't Be a Hero: Have the courage to gracefully retire and let your tag-team mate tackle the dishes.
Yield: 4 sandwiches

"Hulk Hogan's performance in Mr. Nanny gives Nathan Lane a run for his money."
— Mean Gene Okerland

INSIDE SCOOP

There are conflicting stories about how the hoagy got its name. Our favorite is that the sandwich was popularized by the workers on Hog Island, near Philadelphia, where a large shipyard was located. The workers, called "hoggies," brought lunches reflecting their mostly Italian heritage: sandwiches made of crusty bread and cold cuts and flavored with Italian spices. In 1992 the hoagie was voted the official sandwich of Philadelphia. Cheese steak lovers, eat your heart out!

Girls Just Wanna Have Flan

"They just wanna. They just wanna . . ."
—Cyndi Lauper, 1986

You'll Wanna Have:
3 Tbsp citrus zest (i.e. lime, lemon, tangerine)
1/2 cup orange juice
2 cups sugar
2 1/2 cups half & half
1 1/2 cups whole milk
1 vanilla bean, split in half lengthwise
1/2 tsp salt
6 large egg yolks
4 large whole eggs
Trimmed tangerine segments, for garnish
1 cup laughter
1 cup tears

Chew on This

Question: What's the difference between creme caramel, creme renversee, flan and crema caramella?

Answer: The spelling. Whether in French, Spanish or Italian, all these names refer to the same thing: sweetened custard, baked slowly in a caramel-coated mold.

1. Place oven rack in the center of the oven and preheat to 325°F.

2. Cut zest from the citrus being careful to get very little of the bitter white pith.

3. Lay out eight 6-oz custard cups or ramekins and sprinkle a little zest in the bottom of each.

4. Combine the orange juice and 1 cup of the sugar and swirl the pan over medium heat until the sugar dissolves.

5. Once the sugar has dissolved, increase the heat to high and cook without stirring until the syrup first comes to a boil, then begins to turn to a rich amber color, around 8 to 10 minutes.

6. Divide the hot mixture evenly between the custard cups. Tilt and swirl each ramekin (or cup) to evenly coat the sides and bottom with caramel. (Use an oven mitt to do this so you don't burn the you-know-what out of your fingers.)

7. Combine the half & half, whole milk, vanilla bean and salt in a medium size, heavy saucepan over medium heat. Bring to a simmer and remove from the heat.

8. Combine the eggs, egg yolks and the remaining cup of sugar in a large mixing bowl and whisk together until just blended.

9. Remove the vanilla bean from the hot mixture, scraping the edges to release any remaining seeds into the milk. Whisk the hot milk mixture into the egg mixture slowly and gently. Try to create as little foam as possible.

10. Transfer the mixture to a large measuring cup and divide evenly among the zest-and caramel-lined ramekins.

11. Place the ramekins in a large roasting pan or baking dish and set in the oven. Pour enough scalding hot tap water into the pan so that ramekins are two-thirds submerged.

12. Bake anywhere from 45 to 55 minutes until set, but still a little quivery in the center. Cool on a rack and refrigerate at least 2 hours before serving.

13. To serve, dip the bottoms of the ramekins in hot water, slip a paring knife around the sides to loosen and invert ramekins onto plates. Garnish with tangerine segments and zest.

14. After eating your flan, embark on a search for your own mother and when you find her, make her do the dishes.
Yield: 8 servings

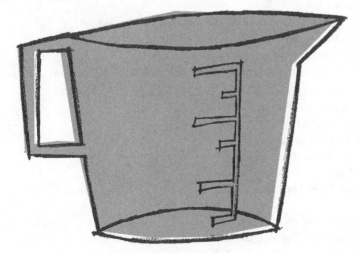

Food for Thought

The first
My Girl was quite
successful, grossing
over $87 million.
At the end of that
movie, Macauley
Culkin dies from a
bee sting. If the
producers of the
movie had known
how popular he
would become, they
probably would
have let him live for
the sequel.

INSIDE SCOOP

Oops! The movie
My Girl 2 is set in
1974. However, a
modern-day
Blockbuster Video™
store can be seen in
the background of
some scenes—quite
out of place, since
VCRs were not widely
available until 1979.

Extraterrestrial Tempura

My Stepmother Is an Alien
(1988)

More mouthwatering than an alien autopsy, more satisfying than a nicely chilled alien probe, more astonishing than a blinding beam of multicolored light hovering above your pickup truck as you drive down a long, dark stretch of deserted highway somewhere north of Las Vegas . . . be prepared to have your tastebuds abducted.

For the Tempura:
8 jumbo shrimp
1 sweet potato, peeled and cut into 1/2 inch rounds
1 yellow onion, halved lengthwise and cut into 1-inch slices
10 medium mushrooms, stems trimmed
1 Japanese eggplant, sliced on the diagonal in 1-inch slices
10 green beans, cleaned and trimmed
1 bunch green onions, trimmed and cut in half
1 canned lotus root, cut on the diagonal into thin slices
  (optional)

For the Dipping Sauce:
1/3 cup sake (or Japanese mirin cooking wine, if available)
1/3 cup light soy sauce
1 cup water
1 cup clam juice (or Japanese dashi, if available)
1 tsp sugar
1 Tbsp fresh ginger, grated
2 Tbsp red radish, grated (or Japanese daikon, if available)

For the Oil and Batter: (makes three batches)
1/2 cup sesame oil
3 cups soy oil
3 egg yolks, beaten
3 cups ice water
3 1/2 cups all-purpose flour
1 copy *Men Are from Mars, Women Are From Venus*

1. Prepare the Shrimp: Shell and devein the shrimp, leaving the tails on. Make 3 or 4 small incisions (1/4 inch) on the inside of each

SCIENCE SAFETY TIP

If your fryer is equipped with a Kleistron tube, never let the oil rise above 360 F. (Ruining a batch of tempura is one thing, but destroying the atmosphere of a neighboring galaxy is universally considered very poor form in anyone's cookbook.)

shrimp to prevent curling as they fry. Rinse in cold water, dry with paper towels, and set aside.

2. Prepare the Vegetables: Dry the cut vegetables well; arrange on a tray or platter.

3. Prepare the Dipping Sauce: In a small saucepan, bring the sake to a boil, ignite with a match and shake gently while the alcohol burns off. Add the soy sauce, water, clam juice, and sugar and return to a boil. Remove from heat, cover and keep warm.

4. Prepare the Oil: In a large, heavy saucepan or deep fryer, combine the sesame and soy oils and heat to a temperature of 340°–360°F. (Test the oil temperature by dripping a few drops of batter into the oil. If the oil is hot enough, the batter will sink partially, then quickly rise to the top.)

5. Prepare the Batter in Three Batches: In a medium mixing bowl, lightly mix 1 egg yolk with 1 cup of the ice water. Add 1 cup of the flour and fold the flour into the egg mixture with just a few strokes until the ingredients are barely combined. Important: The batter should be very lumpy. If mixed until smooth the result will be a thick, heavy coating.

6. Set Up an Assembly Line: Arrange all tools and ingredients from left to right around the cooking area as follows: a) dry shrimp and vegetables; b) remaining sifted flour; c) tempura batter; d) hot oil; e) slotted spoon and chopsticks; f) draining rack or paper towels.

7. Fry the Tempura: Dredge each piece of food to be fried in flour, shake off excess and quickly dip in the batter; fry 2-3 minutes until golden, turning once in the oil. Remove from the oil with a slotted spoon or chopsticks and drain briefly before serving. Use the batter as quickly as possible, mixing more as needed.

8. Eat: Add the ginger and radish to the dipping sauce. Dip each piece of hot and crispy tempura into the sauce and consume. If your mission went as planned, it should be as crisp as a crop circle and taste out of this world.

Yield: 2 servings

ALIEN TIP #224

Whether you're a resident of Earth or just a visitor, you should check out the International U.F.O. Museum and Research Center in Roswell, New Mexico. (Phone # is: 800-822-3545)

Food for Thought

As an advanced being from an alien culture, why does Kim Basinger still have to carry a purse?

Bluto's Beer Chili

You're invited to join the Delta house for one rousing, out-of-control chili recipe made with plenty of ice-cold beer. Don't worry, though, most of the alcohol burns off during cooking so you won't land on double-secret probation.

3 Tbsp corn oil
2 lbs skirt steak, cut into 1/2-inch cubes
2 lbs pork sausage
10 cloves garlic, peeled and minced
2 medium onions, coarsely chopped
2 jalapeño peppers, seeded and finely diced
2 Tbsp ground cumin
1 Tbsp ground coriander
5 Tbsp chili powder
1 Tbsp paprika
1 tsp chili flakes
2 tsp oregano
1 tsp sage
1 bell pepper, diced
2 stalks celery, diced
1 28-oz can crushed tomatoes (retain liquid)
1 6-oz can roasted chilies, blended or finely chopped
2 cups beef stock
1 bay leaf
2 tsp salt
4 cups pinto or black beans, fully cooked (optional)
2 Tbsp fine cornmeal or masa harina (optional)
8 25-gal kegs of beer, ice cold . . . okay, 2 12-oz cans of beer
  (can't blame a guy for trying!)

1. In a large cast-iron skillet, heat the oil over medium-high heat until quite hot. Lightly brown the meat, in three or four batches, to avoid overcrowding the skillet.

2. Transfer the browned meat to a large Dutch oven or heavy casserole. Discard all but 3 tablespoons of fat from the skillet.

DID YOU KNOW?

Founded in 1970 by veterans of the *Harvard Lampoon* humor magazine, *National Lampoon* thrust countercultural humor into the face of the masses, championing a "no-sacred-cows" philosophy that left no one safe from parody. Perhaps the most infamous *NL* cover photo featured a dog with a gun to its head, with the headline "Buy this Magazine or We'll Kill this Dog."

3. Reduce skillet heat to medium and add the garlic, onion and diced jalapeño pepper. Sauté for 2 minutes, stirring often.

4. Add the cumin, coriander, chili powder, paprika, chili flakes, oregano and sage to the skillet; stirring well to coat the onions, garlic and jalapeños with the spices.

5. Continue cooking the spice mixture for another minute, stirring frequently to avoid scorching.

6. Add the bell pepper, celery, crushed tomatoes with their juice, and the canned chilies. Stir well with a wooden spoon, scraping the bottom and sides to loosen any tasty bits stuck to the skillet. Transfer contents of the skillet to the Dutch oven and place over medium-high heat.

7. Add the beef stock, bay leaf and beer to the Dutch oven, stirring well to mix all the ingredients.

8. Bring the chili to a boil. Reduce the heat to low and with the pot half covered, cook at a simmer 1-2 hours, until the meat is tender.

9. If you are adding beans: When the meat is tender, add the cooked beans and simmer another 20 minutes. Warm beans may also be held on the side and added by request.

Note: If you want the chili to be a little thicker, add 2 tablespoons of the corn meal or masa harina a little at a time, stirring constantly. This will thicken the chili up some and add a subtle, earthy flavor. Yield: 12-16 servings (enough for the whole frat)

INSIDE SCOOP

This marks the film debut of our favorite actor with food in his name, Kevin Bacon.

Chew on This

BEAN TIP #237

The process of soaking dried beans overnight before cooking helps eliminate the compounds that cause audible gastrointestinal turbulence. During Delta pledge week, please disregard.

Road Trip Tri-Tip

Life on the road can leave you with a hunger the size of The Giant Ball of Twine. Especially after unexpected detours to The House of Mud, Fluker's Worm Farm and Ye Olde Trailer Park O' Trashy Relatives. Keep up your strength with a juicy barbecue sandwich that's spicy enough to stop highway hypnosis and get you back on the road to wherever it is you're going.

TRI-TIP TIP

Practically unknown outside of California, the tri-tip wasn't popular until the early 1950s. A Santa Maria butcher reserved the triangular shaped tip of the bottom sirloin usually doomed to be ground into hamburger. He slow-roasted it, gave samples to his customers and called it tri-tip. And the rest is meat history.

For the Sauce:
2 Tbsp butter
1 medium onion, diced
4 cloves garlic, peeled and finely chopped
1 tsp dry mustard
4 Tbsp brown sugar
1 tsp instant coffee
1-2 Tbsp hot pepper sauce
2 cups tomato sauce
1/2 cup cider vinegar
Salt and pepper to taste

For the Slaw:
4 Tbsp almond slivers, toasted
1/4 cup olive oil
2 Tbsp toasted sesame oil
3 Tbsp lemon juice
1/2 tsp mustard seed
1/2 tsp celery seed
1/2 head red cabbage, thinly sliced
2 ripe tomatoes, diced
3 ears fresh corn, cut from the cob
3 scallions, thinly sliced
Salt and black pepper to taste
Un-foldable road maps, ancient flares
   and the most current hours of operation for Walley World

Chew on This

Part of the original cast of "Saturday Night Live," Chevy Chase left the show to pursue a movie career after just one season. SNL had lasting effects on Chase, though—he developed a chronic back problem from all the pratfalls he took on that show.

For the Tri-Tip sandwiches:
1 2-3 lb Beef tri-tip or sirloin tip roast
1 Tbsp each: ground black pepper, ground oregano, ground
  cumin, celery salt, garlic powder and paprika
4 large, seeded hamburger buns

1. Fasten your seat-belts, check the mirrors and preheat the oven to 350°F.

2. **"Are we there yet?"** In a small bowl, combine the black pepper, oregano, cumin, celery salt, garlic powder and paprika.

3. Rub the spice mix well into the meat and place the roast fat-side up in a foil-lined pan. Bake for 45 minutes to an hour, or until the internal temperature in the thickest part of the meat reads 120°-125°F.

4. **"Are we there yet?"** While the tri-tip cooks, make the BBQ sauce. In a medium saucepan, over medium heat, melt the butter and sauté the onions and garlic until soft and golden.

5. Add the mustard, brown sugar and instant coffee to the saucepan and cook for one minute, stirring constantly.

6. Stir in the hot pepper sauce, tomato sauce and vinegar. When the mixture comes to a boil, reduce the heat and simmer 30 minutes. Check and adjust seasonings.

7. Remove the meat from the oven and let rest a few minutes before slicing thinly across the grain and returning to the roasting pan.

8. Slather the meat with plenty of warm sauce and return to the oven, then prepare the slaw.

9. **"Are we there yet?"** In a large bowl, mix almonds, olive oil, sesame oil, lemon juice, mustard seed and celery seed. Add the chopped cabbage, tomatoes, corn and scallions. Season to taste with salt and pepper. Toss and refrigerate until serving.

10. **"We're there!"** Heat the buns, pile high with barbecued beef, smother with gobs of warm sauce and arrange entire meal precariously onto flimsy paper plates. Hop into the family wagon (beginning, yet again, another rousing chorus of "99 Bottles of Beer on the Wall") and get back on the open road, secure in the knowledge that your upholstery will never, ever look the same again.
Yield: 4 servings

INSIDE SCOOP

The Griswold's original vacation destination was scripted as Disneyland, but it was changed to the fictitious Walley World when Disney objected, arguing that they are open 365 days a year. *Vacation's* Walley World was closed for repairs when the Griswolds arrived.

Sergeant Foley's Drop and Give Me 20-Bean Salad
(topped with Moody and Misunderstood Zack Mayo)

Sound off, soldiers!
I don't know but I been told!
Eskimo Pies are really cold!
I don't know but I been taught!
Julia Child's really hot!

Chew on This

Louis Gossett, Jr.'s
role in this film
won him an Oscar®
for Best Supporting
Actor and became
the definitive
portrait of the
hard-nosed drill
sergeant, inspiring
innumerable
imitators through
the years.

For the Zack Mayo:
2 egg yolks
1/2 tsp Dijon mustard
1/2 tsp salt
2 Tbsp chives, chopped
2 Tbsp fresh dill, chopped
1 Tbsp fresh chervil
1 tsp red wine vinegar
1 1/2 cups canola oil
2 Tbsp lemon juice

For the 20-Bean Salad:
4 eggs
4 small red potatoes
10 green beans, trimmed
10 yellow wax beans, trimmed
3 large tomatoes, quartered
1 can oil-packed, solid white tuna
1/2 cup brine-cured olives
1/4 cup toasted almonds
1 head Boston or Bibb lettuce
1 large chip on shoulder

D&aM SEAL OF APPROVAL

This movie gets extra
points for naming the
main character after our
favorite condiment,
mayonnaise.

1. You eyeballin' me, boy?: Combine egg yolks, mustard, salt, chives, dill, chervil and vinegar in the work bowl of a food processor.

2. Process at high speed while adding the oil a few drops at a time. Add the lemon juice and correct seasonings to taste. Cover and refrigerate.

3. You're not worthy to boil the eggs!: Place the eggs in a medium saucepan and cover with cold water. Bring to a boil, remove from heat, cover and let stand for 25 minutes. Peel and quarter when cool enough to handle.

4. Prep the veggies . . . Now prep them again, AND DO IT RIGHT!: Fill a small saucepan with cold water and a pinch of salt, slice the potatoes into slices 1/4-inch thick, dropping the slices into the water as you work.

5. Bring the potatoes to a simmer and cook 3 to 4 minutes, until tender. Drain, toss with a few drops of olive oil and refrigerate.

6. Cook the beans in lightly salted boiling water until tender, about 5 minutes. Immediately refresh by plunging into ice water until cool to the touch.

7. You're never gonna get through this salad, why don't you quit now and make it easy on everyone: Arrange lettuce on plates and top decoratively with the eggs, potatoes, beans, tuna, tomatoes, olives and almonds.

8. We suggest serving the dressing on the side. (Not everyone can tolerate the same amount of Zack Mayo.)

Tip: Wait until it's time to do the dishes, then dramatically announce you've decided to D.O.R. and head for the hills. Dis-Missed!

Yield: 4 servings

Food for Thought

Richard Gere owes John Travolta for three big breaks in his career. *Days of Heaven*, *American Gigolo* and *An Officer and a Gentleman* were all turned down by Travolta before being offered to Gere.

INSIDE SCOOP

The inspiration for our "Drop and Give Me 20-Bean Salad" was of course that archetypal buffet treat of the '50s, the three-bean salad. Said to have been invented by the good people at Stokely-Van Kamp, the original recipe featured one can each of green, yellow and kidney beans and was proudly touted as "The Salad Men Love."

Irish Stew for One

Mom hate your girlfriend? Girlfriend hate your mom? Take the high road, curl up with a cup of Irish Stew for One and ponder the joys of the single serving. You'll never sit by the phone waiting for YOU to call, you'll never have to dress for dinner and when you ask YOURSELF that age-old question, "Will you respect me in the morning?" only YOU will know the answer. To paraphrase our infamous former surgeon general, Jocelyn Elders, "Help yourself!"

For the Stew:
2 lbs lamb shoulder, cut into 1–2-inch cubes
2 Tbsp olive oil
2 cups chicken stock, beef stock or water
2 each: bay leaf, thyme sprig, garlic clove
4 medium potatoes, peeled and sliced
2 yellow onions, peeled and sliced
1 carrot, sliced
3 Tbsp parsley, chopped
1 10-oz can cannellini beans
Salt and pepper

For the Soda Bread:
2 cups flour
1 tsp salt
1/2 tsp baking soda
1 tsp rosemary, chopped
1 cup buttermilk
2 Tbsp tomato paste
1 copy "How to Be Your Own Best Friend"

1. Take a quick peek at your date book . . . anything on for tonight? . . . if not, proceed to step 2.

2. Preheat oven to 250°F.

3. Prepare the Stew: Heat the oil in a large Dutch oven or a heavy pot over medium-high heat.

4. Brown the meat in 3 batches, then return all the meat to the pot and

Chew on This

This recipe, like most long-cooked stews, is best if cooked the day before you want to eat it.

add the stock, bay leaf, thyme and garlic. Season with salt and pepper.

5. Bring to a simmer, cover and bake 30 minutes.

6. Meanwhile, cut the vegetables. (You obviously have nothing else to do, loser.)

7. Add the potatoes, onions, carrot, cannellini beans and chopped parsley. Cover and continue cooking until the vegetables are tender, about 20 minutes.

8. Prepare the Soda Bread: Meanwhile, make some Irish soda bread. (Unless you've got plans for later? . . . didn't think so.) Preheat the oven to 375°F.

9. Combine the flour, salt, baking soda and rosemary in a mixing bowl.

10. In a small bowl, mix together the tomato paste and the buttermilk.

11. Add the buttermilk mixture to the flour mixture and knead just until the dough holds together.

12. Shape the dough into small, depressing, 1-person loaves and brush with a little olive oil. Bake about 15-20 minutes, or until done.

13. Set the table and get ready to party.

Yield: MAKES ONE LARGE, LONELY SERVING

Food for Thought

This movie was loosely based on the 1955 classic film, Marty, which won Academy Awards™ for Best Picture and Best Actor for star Ernest Borgnine.

INSIDE SCOOP

John Candy won Emmy® awards in 1982 and 1983 for his writing on the influential comedy show "SCTV." Candy's memorable characters on that show included: accordion whiz Yosh Schmenge of the polka duo The Schmenge Brothers and Dr. Tongue, the hulking star of late-night "Monster Chiller Horror Theater."

"Pony Boy" Fries and "Cherry Valence" Pie

In this stylized Francis Ford Coppola production of S. E. Hinton's brooding tale, truants are living on their own and on the run. Lucky for us, you don't have to be a runaway to enjoy this Classic Unsupervised Adolescent Fare.®

For the Pie Crust:
2 1/2 cups flour
1/2 tsp salt
1 Tbsp sugar
6 Tbsp chilled
  vegetable shortening,
  cut into 1/4-inch cubes
8 Tbsp chilled unsalted butter,
  cut into 1/4-inch cubes
5-7 Tbsp ice water

For the Pie Filling:
1 tsp freshly ground cinnamon
1 cup sugar
2 Tbsp cornstarch
2 Tbsp quick-cooking tapioca
4-5 cups sour cherries, drained
1/2 cup cherry juice
1/8 tsp almond extract
1 Tbsp fresh lemon juice
2 Tbsp butter

For the Fries:
5 mature russet potatoes
Canola oil, as needed
Salt
Chili powder
1 switchblade-style pie knife
1 copy *Gone With the Wind*

Chew on This

Never eat a lot of fries right before participating in a big rumble. They'll just slow you down and you'll need your teeth later for eating that cherry pie.

1. Pie Crust: Preheat over to 450°F. In a medium bowl, combine the flour, salt, and sugar. Add the shortening, using a pastry blender or two knives to work it into the flour until it resembles coarse cornmeal. Cut in butter until the bits are no larger than small peas.

2. Sprinkle ice water onto the mixture one tablespoon at a time, mixing with a fork after each addition to moisten the dough evenly. The amount of ice water needed may vary accordingly. Using your hands, gently shape the dough into 2 balls; then flatten into 5-inch discs. Wrap in plastic and refrigerate for 30 minutes.

3. For the Filling: Mix together the cinnamon, sugar, cornstarch, and tapioca. Add the cherries, cherry juice, almond extract and lemon juice. Let stand 10 minutes.

4. Assemble the Pie: Roll out one piece of chilled dough to approximately 10 inches in diameter. Transfer dough to a buttered 9-inch pie plate and trim edges to leave 1/2-inch excess. Fold excess under itself. Lightly brush the inside of the crust with egg white. Pour filling into crust and dot with butter.

5. Roll out remaining pastry dough and cut into 1-inch-wide strips. Lay strips over the filling in a criss-cross latticework. Trim excess, fold under, and flute the edges with a fork.

6. Bake for 10 minutes in the lower third of the oven, reduce heat to 350°F, and continue baking another 45 minutes until the crust is golden brown.

7. Make the Fries: Scrub potatoes, peel (optional), and cut into strips 3 inches long and 3/8-inch square. Cover with cold water and let stand 10-20 minutes. Drain and dry well with paper towels.

8. Fill deep-fat fryer or large saucepan with oil to a depth of 5-6 inches. Using a frying thermometer, slowly heat to a temperature of 300°–325°F.

9. Fry potatoes in one-to two-cup batches until they begin to turn a pale gold, about 2 minutes. Remove from oil with a slotted spoon and drain on paper towels in a single layer until cool to the touch.

10. Raise oil temperature to 375°F and refry the blanched potatoes in small batches, moving them constantly until crisp and golden, about 3 minutes. (When no one is looking, take a minute and whisper to them "Stay crisp and golden, man.") Drain, toss with salt and chili powder, and serve at once.
Yield: 8 servings

Food for Thought

POTATO FACTS
#12 & #13

Potatoes are by far the most popular vegetable in the United States and, in many parts of the world, French fries are called American fries.

Bridget Fondue

Point of No Return is a remake of the popular French action movie, *La Femme Nikita* directed by Luc Resson. Both films feature a beautiful sociopath re-trained to be a government assassin. Like our heroine, this Bridget Fondue is hot, enticing and dangerous and will no doubt inspire its own imitators.

1 clove garlic, peeled
1 Tbsp butter
1 1/2 pounds Swiss cheese
3 Tbsp flour
1 cup champagne
1/2 tsp white pepper
1 pinch cayenne pepper
1 pinch nutmeg
1/2 tsp lemon zest
1/2 cup green olives, thinly sliced
1 ounce vodka
1 French bread or baguette
1 top-secret spy watch that converts to a handy whisk watch
Killer instincts

DID YOU KNOW?
Fondue was originally created by European goatherders to use up stale bread and old cheese.

IDEA FOR A NETWORK:

NIKITAVISION! Programming consists entirely of the movies *La Femme Nikita*, and *Point of No Return*, the TV show, *La Femme Nikita* and old news footage of Nikita Kruschev.

1. Grate or chop the cheese as finely as possible, toss with the flour and set aside.

2. Rub inside of fondue pot or earthenware casserole with the clove of garlic, then the butter.

3. Place the pot over medium heat, add the champagne and heat until just boiling.

4. Add the floured cheese a handful at a time, stirring with a wooden spoon after each addition.

5. When the cheese is melted and creamy, add the white pepper, cayenne, nutmeg, lemon zest and olives.

6. When the fondue comes to a boil, stir in the vodka.

7. Cut the French bread into small cubes (preferably so that each cube has one crusty edge), spear savagely with your weapon of choice and dispatch without mercy.

10. When dinner's over, call the cleaner and hope it's not Harvey Keitel. Yield: 6 servings

FONDUES & DONT'S

According to a highly-placed source at the CIA's Fondue Training Center in Langely, VA, if your bread falls off its fork into the fondue pot, you're required to kiss the person to your right (or is it your left? we keep forgetting). Anyway, kiss the one who looks more like Bridget Fonda or Gabriel Byrne (if dining alone, see p.114 for *Only The Lonely*). If you doubt there's a CIA Fondue Training Center, just ask yourself, "Why IS there government cheese?"

INSIDE SCOOP

Point of No Return star Bridget Fonda is the daughter of actor Peter Fonda, the granddaughter of actor Henry Fonda and the niece of the fantastically beautiful and talented actress Jane Fonda who just happens to be married to our boss, Ted Turner. Did we mention she's fantastically beautiful and talented AND BRILLIANT? Over the past 60 years, the acting Fondas have collectively starred in over 250 films.

Julia's Angel Hair Puttanesca

Pretty Woman (1990)

In this 1990 inspirational Cinderella story, Julia Robert's stunning debut made quite an impression on young girls everywhere. Her realistic portrayal of a beautiful, bright-eyed, healthy, well-adjusted prostitute proved not only that profit and passion do go hand in hand, but also gave the oldest profession a well-needed boost.

1/3 cup extra-virgin olive oil
1 onion, peeled and chopped
1 carrot, cut into small dice
4 garlic cloves, peeled and minced
6 anchovy filets, rinsed and mashed
1/4 tsp crushed red pepper
1/2 cup dry red wine
3 lbs ripe tomatoes or 1 28-oz can peeled plum tomatoes,
   drained and chopped
1 1/2 cups flavorful black olives, pitted and halved
3 Tbsp large capers, drained
Salt and pepper
1 lb angel hair pasta
Hugh Grant's phone number

TOMATO TIPS
#87 & #88
Never store tomatoes in the refrigerator for any length of time. Cold temperatures hurt both the texture and the flavor. If ripe tomatoes aren't available, never hesitate to use good-quality canned Italian plum tomatoes.

1. Heat the olive oil in a medium saucepan over medium-low heat. Add the onion and carrot and cook very slowly until the onion becomes soft and translucent, about 10 minutes. Add the garlic, anchovies, and crushed red pepper; continue cooking until the garlic just begins to turn golden. (Don't let it brown.)

2. Add the red wine and raise the heat to medium-high. Simmer until the wine is almost completely reduced. Stir in the tomatoes, olives, and capers. Reduce heat to medium and cook uncovered for 20 minutes, stirring often. (While the sauce simmers, bring 5-6 quarts of water to a boil in a large pot or Dutch oven.)

3. When the sauce has thickened, stir in the chopped parsley and season to taste with salt and pepper. Add more red pepper flakes if desired.

4. When the water boils, add 2 tablespoons of salt and return to a boil. Add the pasta and stir immediately to prevent sticking. Cover the pot until the water returns to a boil again; then remove cover and cook until pasta is *al dente*, stirring often.

5. Drain pasta into a colander over a large pasta bowl. Pour the water out and wipe the bowl with a towel before transferring the pasta to the warmed bowl. Immediately ladle the sauce over the pasta. Toss and serve in shallow bowls.

Yield: 4-6 servings

Chew on This

Prostitution is illegal in the U.S. except in certain counties in Nevada, not including Reno or Las Vegas.

INSIDE SCOOP

It's no secret the famous Italian dish, *Puttanesca*, is derived from the Italian *puttana* for "whore." There is some disagreement, however, on how it got the name. Some say the irresistible and alluring fragrance of this sauce is the reason. We prefer another story that suggests it was the speed in which the sauce could be cooked that made it a clear favorite among those who needed to get back to business. "Check, please!"

Extra Cheesy Spielburgers

Raiders of the Lost Ark
(1981)

Rumor has it that Steven Spielberg is a "Dinner & a Movie" fan. And Steven, we're big fans of yours. Hey, we work on a cooking show. Knowing which side our bread is buttered on is practically our business. We like Steven, he likes us, we'll send him one of those 14 action-packed, food-adventure scripts we've got in our bottom drawer.

As long as you're here, let me pitch this . . . it all starts when a TV chef discovers a mystical golden strainer empowered with the ability to separate good from evil . . .

Starring (in order of appearance):
2 lbs either beef chuck, top round, chicken or turkey thighs
  or lean lamb, very cold
1/4 cup crushed ice
1/4 cup scallions, chopped
2 Tbsp parsley, chopped
1 tsp freshly cracked black pepper
Kosher salt to taste
1 lb sharp cheddar, thinly sliced
2 Tbsp butter
2 cups mushrooms, sliced
2 Tbsp peanut oil
1 beefsteak tomato, sliced
1 white onion, peeled and thinly sliced
1 small head romaine lettuce
Condiments galore
4 buns (plus 2 bun stand-ins)
1 "King of the World" Club membership card

1. Pre-Production: After casting the role of "leading meat" for your extravaganza, contact the representing agent and begin negotiations. (Scale plus 10% and a few points on the meal should secure the deal.) Cut the meat into 1-2-inch pieces and transfer to a food processor. Add the crushed ice and using short pulses, grind the meat to the consistency of coarse hamburger. Don't over grind (or over direct) or the meat will become tough. Transfer to a mixing bowl, add the scallions, parsley and black pepper; mix together well.

2. Divide the meat into 4 equal pieces. Form each piece into a virtual blockbuster of a burger, each one more fantastic and wildly successful than the one before it. (If really aspiring to greatness, try forming the patties around a fat chunk of cheese . . . who cares if it throws you over budget and behind schedule, this is your vision, dammit!) Season both sides of the patties with kosher salt and refrigerate.

3. Sauté the mushrooms in butter (assuring them privately all the while that they are the *real* stars of this meal.) Season with salt and pepper and set aside.

4. Production: Heat a heavy, cast-iron skillet over medium-high heat until very hot. Quickly brush the pan with peanut oil and ask the assistant director to call for the patties.

5. After the patties have walked through the blocking and are comfortable with their motivations, shout "ACTION!" and thrust them into the pan. The scene should last about 4 minutes; flip them and do the reversals, then top each burger with as much cheese as you can get away with.

6. Continue working until each burger is cooked precisely the way you want it . . . if you want 'rare', yell "CUT" now! . . . if you feel 'medium' will help skew a larger, younger audience, then continue cooking 2 minutes longer.

7. Smother each burger with sautéed mushrooms and excruciatingly obsequious accolades (making a mental note to phone their agent and kvetch about how impossible they were to work with.)

8. Post-Production: Give yourself a pat on the back and exit stage right before someone directs you to do the dishes.
Yield: 4 servings

INSIDE SCOOP

The famous moment in which Indy responds to a knife-wielding marauder by unceremoniously shooting him was not in the original script. Suffering from dysentery, Harrison Ford was impatient to end the day's filming and improvised this legendary scene.

Chew on This

No one disputes that the hamburger was named for the famous seaport town of Hamburg, Germany. However, the first U.S. appearance of this quintessentially American, bun-encased, hand-held banquet is a subject of sizzling debate. Although many food historians theorize burgers were born during the 1904 St. Louis World's Fair-Louisiana Purchase exposition, we decided to resolve this once and for all. Alas, after a sea of condiments and countless root beers, we were too bloated and sleepy to reach an official consensus.

Real Men's Quiche

Real Men
(1987)

Who cares if real men don't eat quiche? It takes a real man to make one entirely from scratch, especially when being chased by Soviet agents.

For the Shell:
1 1/2 cups all-purpose flour
1/2 tsp salt
1 tsp sugar
4 oz butter, chilled and cut into pieces
2 Tbsp vegetable shortening, chilled
1 large egg, chilled
3 Tbsp ice water

For the Filling:
4 eggs
1 1/2 cups half-and-half
1 tsp red pepper flakes
1/2 tsp black pepper
1/2 tsp oregano
1/2 tsp salt
1/4 cup fresh basil, chopped
1 cup hot Italian sausage, cooked and crumbled
1 7-oz can roasted chilies, thinly sliced
1/2 cup Jack cheese, shredded
1 cup cheddar cheese, shredded
1 ripe tomato, thinly sliced
1 fully loaded index finger (silencer optional)

1. Be a Man and Make the Shell Yourself: Preheat the oven to 425°F. In the bowl of a food processor, combine the flour, salt, sugar, and butter. Pulse 4 times to combine the ingredients. Add the butter, shortening, and the egg and pulse the machine 5-6 more times until the dough resembles small peas. Add the ice water and pulse again. Scrape dough out onto a clean work surface and knead once or twice by hand. Shape into a 5-inch disc; wrap in plastic and refrigerate for at least 20 minutes.

Chew on This

Real Men star John Ritter is the son of singing country stars Tex Ritter and Dorothy Fay.

2. Roll It Out and Bake It (if you can take it): Roll out the dough evenly to a diameter of approximately 13 inches. Turn an 8-inch cake pan upside down and butter all surfaces. Transfer the dough to the outside surface of the pan and trim any overhanging edges. Flute the edges with the tines of a fork. Bake upside for 10 minutes.

3. Remove from oven and cool at least 15 minutes before inverting and removing the cake pan from the pastry shell.

4. Get a Little Rough: In a mixing bowl, combine the eggs, half-and-half, pepper flakes, black pepper, oregano, salt, and basil. Beat well.

5. Fill It Up: Place the shell on a cooking sheet. Sprinkle the sausage and one-half of each cheese into the pastry shell. Fill with the egg mixture to 1/4-inch of the rim and arrange the roasted chilies on top. Reduce the oven temperature to 375°F.

6. Can You Take the Heat?: Sprinkle quiche with remaining cheese and arrange the tomato slices over the top. Bake for about 40 minutes, until puffy and nicely browned.

7. Cut into slices and stand proudly with arms akimbo while your adoring guests enjoy the meal.
Yield: 6-8 servings

INSIDE SCOOP
When making any type of pie shell handle the dough as little as possible. Over kneading increases the gluten structure and can make the pastry tough.

Tommy's Tighty Whitey Whitefish

(with Oh So Satisfying Sauce Mornay)

Tom Cruise slid onto the scene in his Ray Bans™ and form-fitting white briefs and the world would never be the same. He made free enterprise look sexy and gave the oldest profession a brand-new spin. This white fish is another refreshing update of an old recipe and, like Tommy, is best enjoyed covered in a creamy Sauce De Mornay.

1 cup whole milk
1/2 cup clam juice
1/2 small onion
2 cloves
1/2 small bay leaf
2 Tbsp butter
3 Tbsp flour
Salt, pepper and nutmeg to taste
1 1/2 Tbsp gruyere cheese, grated
1 1/2 Tbsp Parmesan cheese, grated
4 8-oz filets white fish, salmon, halibut, tilefish or any
   other firm, fresh, supple, white, fleshed fish
2 Tbsp olive oil
1 leek, cut into matchstick-sized pieces
4 mushrooms, thinly sliced
1 carrot, peeled and cut into matchstick-sized pieces
1 red bell pepper, cut into matchstick-sized pieces
The house to yourself

1. Make the Sauce Mornay: Preheat the oven to 450°F. Combine the milk, clam juice, onion, clove and bay leaf in a small saucepan over medium heat and bring to a simmer.

2. In a second, small saucepan over low heat, gently melt the butter. Using a wooden spoon, stir in the flour a little at a time, increase the heat to medium and cook for about 3 minutes. Remove the pan from the heat to cool for a minute.

3. Strain the milk mixture into a small bowl and discard the solids.

4. Slowly whisk the hot milk into the butter and flour mixture; return the mixture to a medium heat and return to a simmer, whisking rapidly.

5. Reduce the heat to low and continue to simmer 30 minutes, skimming the surface occasionally.

6. Add and stir in the cheeses, season to taste and keep warm until use.

7. Make the Fish: Heat the olive oil in a large skillet over medium-low heat and sauté the vegetables without browning, about 5 minutes. Set aside.

8. Cut 4 pieces of parchment paper or foil into pieces 12-inches square.

9. Place a piece of fish on each sheet of parchment and cover with small ladle of Mornay sauce. Top each piece with the matchstick vegetable mixture.

10. Seal the contents into tighty-white packages by making a series of folds all around the edges. Place in a shallow baking dish.

11. Bake for about 15 minutes, until the fish is opaque and flaky.

12. Put on your favorite old-time rock n' roll album, don your coolest shades and slide into the dining room.

13. These tighty-white packages should be opened right at the table. (For safety's sake, allow the steam to escape before digging in.)
Yield: 4 servings

INSIDE SCOOP

In the script for this film, the only direction for the famous underwear scene is: "Joel dances in living room". The underwear and Ray Bans™ came courtesy of Tom Cruise himself.

Chew on This

At age 14, Tom Cruise entered a seminary, supposedly intending to enter the priesthood. He left after one year.

Swayze's Cracked Ribs and Black-eyed Peas

Roadhouse
(1989)

In this 1989 classic—and we do mean classic—Patrick Swayze plays that rarest of triple hyphenates: Zen Master-Philosopher-Bar Room Bouncer. His favorite dish may be a knuckle sandwich, but we'll take cracked ribs and black-eyed peas any day.

Ribs and Rub:
5 lbs pork ribs, cracked
2 quarts beer
2 cups cider vinegar
1 Tbsp each: freshly ground
  black pepper, ground
  oregano, ground cumin
2 Tbsp each: celery salt,
  brown sugar and chili powder
3 Tbsp each: garlic powder
  and paprika

Black-eyed Peas:
1 yellow onion, peeled and diced
2 cloves garlic
1 carrot, diced
1 celery stalk, diced
1 10-oz package frozen black-eyed peas (or fresh
  if available)
1 bay leaf
2 cups chicken stock
Salt and pepper to taste
A good health plan

Moppin' Sauce:
2 Tbsp butter
1 medium onion, diced
4 cloves garlic,
  finely chopped
1 tsp dry mustard
4 Tbsp brown sugar
1 tsp instant coffee
1-3 Tbsp hot pepper sauce
2 cups tomato sauce
1/2 cup cider vinegar
Salt and pepper to taste

Chew on This

The word "barbecue" comes from the French, "barbe a queue" which means "from the whiskers to the tail."

1. Preheat oven to 425°F. Place the ribs in a large pot over high heat and cover with the beer, vinegar and just enough water to completely cover the ribs. As soon as the water begins to boil, remove the pot from the heat, cover and set aside for 20 minutes.

2. The Moppin' Sauce: In a medium saucepan, over medium heat, melt the butter and sauté the onions and garlic until soft and golden.

3. Add the mustard, brown sugar and instant coffee to the saucepan and cook for one minute, stirring constantly.

4. Stir in the hot sauce, tomato sauce and vinegar. When the mixture comes to a boil, reduce the heat and simmer 30-45 minutes. Season to taste with salt and black pepper.

5. The Rub: Mix the dry rub ingredients. Remove the ribs from the pot and rub well with the dry rub mixture.

6. Place the ribs fat-side up in a foil-lined pan and bake for 40 minutes, turning once halfway through cooking.

7. Reduce the heat to 350°F. Pour the fat from the pan, reserving 2 tablespoons, and cover the ribs with hot sauce. Wrap well in foil and bake until tender, about 45 minutes.

8. The Black-eyed peas: In a medium saucepan, sauté the onion and garlic in the reserved rib drippings until lightly golden.

9. Add the carrot, celery, peas, bay leaf and chicken stock; bring to a boil. Reduce heat and cook until the beans are tender, about 30 minutes. Season to taste with salt and pepper.

10. Macho Zen Observation: Cracked ribs may not hurt, but they sure do taste good.

Yield: 4 servings

INSIDE SCOOP

Speaking of cracked ribs...in the course of his various athletic pursuits—football, gymnastics, ice skating and dancing—Patrick Swayze has broken his ankle and all 10 fingers, and had 5 operations on his left knee.

"Pain don't hurt."
—Patrick Swayze as Dalton in the movie *Roadhouse*

Tony Manero's Mozzarella Marinara

Saturday Night Fever (1977)

The year was 1977. You had a different date every Saturday night. You could eat plate after plate of deep-fried cheese in little Italian restaurants into the wee hours. You could wear white polyester and still feel good about yourself.

Times have changed. We watch our cholesterol and the last thing we want on a Saturday night is a fever. Well, we can't help you with your love life or your fashion sense, but we can offer you this example of Heart Smart Disco Fare® that may help keep you ha, ha, ha, ha stayin' alive.

For the Marinara:
1 28-oz can Italian plum tomatoes, cut in quarters
2 Tbsp extra-virgin olive oil
3 anchovy filets, chopped
2 cloves garlic, peeled and thinly sliced
Chopped parsley
Freshly ground black pepper

Food for Thought

Elvis died the year
*Saturday Night
Fever* was released.

For the Mozzarella:
6 sheets frozen filo dough (also spelled phyllo and fillo), defrosted
3 Tbsp extra-virgin olive oil
12 1-oz packages part-skim mozzarella (also labeled string cheese)
1 cup bread crumbs
1/4 cup finely shredded fresh basil
Whole fresh basil leaves for garnish
1 disco ball

Chew on This

The soundtrack for
*Saturday Night
Fever*, along with
that of *Grease*, is in
the list of 5 top
grossing sound-
tracks of all time.

1. Prepare for a Hot Night: Preheat oven to 325°F. In a large mixing bowl, combine the tomatoes, olive oil, anchovies, and garlic. Spread out the contents of the bowl on a large cookie sheet and roast for 30 minutes, stirring once or twice. Transfer to the work bowl of a food processor or blender. Pulse quickly 3-4 times. The sauce should be somewhat chunky. Season with chopped parsley and freshly ground black pepper to taste. Cover and keep warm.

2. Dress Up the Mozzarella: Increase the oven temperature to 375°F. Lay out 1 piece of filo on a clean, dry surface. (Keep the remaining pieces covered with a damp cloth until use or they will dry out and crack.) Cut 2 strips, 6-7 inches wide from the first sheet. Lay the strips side by side and brush both sides of each strip lightly with olive oil.

3. Sprinkle 1 tablespoon of bread crumbs and 1/2 teaspoon of basil evenly over the top of each strip. Center 1 piece of cheese at the end of the filo strip closest to you and roll up tightly. The filo-wrapped cheese should resemble a small cigar. Fold the ends under, sprinkle with bread crumbs, and place on an ungreased baking sheet. Repeat process for each piece of the remaining cheese. Bake for 10 minutes until "cigars" are hot and crispy.

4. Strut Your Stuff: Lay out 6 warmed plates and make a pool of marinara in the center of each. Place 2 mozzarella "cigars" over the sauce and garnish with a basil leaf.
Yield: 6 servings

"I remember the old days at the five-four . . . no shoes, no shirts, lots of service. . ."
—Larry, "Dinner & a Movie"'s Ubiquitous Appliance Guy and Studio 54's smoke machine repairman

OLIVE OIL FACT #57

Olive oil is made up of nearly 75 percent monounsaturated fat, the type of fat that actually helps to lower high cholesterol levels in the body. It also contains elements believed to prevent cancer and slow the aging process. Some say it also aids in the ability to learn complex dance routines.

Pecan Someone Your Own Size Pie

Sleeping with the Enemy
(1991)

Those eyes, that mouth, that utter defenselessness . . . when you see Julia Roberts there's just one thing you wanna do. Feed her pie. That's right, our favorite Southern dish . . . for our favorite Southern dish.

Maybe pie can't solve all the world's problems, but, doggonit, it's a good place to start. "Dinner & a Movie", Healing the World One Pie at a Time®.

For the Pie Shell:
1 1/2 cups all-purpose flour
2 Tbsp ground pecans
1/2 tsp salt
2 Tbsp sugar
4 Tbsp cold shortening, cut into pieces
6 Tbsp butter, cut into pieces
1 egg, separated
2 tsp cold milk

For the Filling:
3 eggs, at room temperature
6 Tbsp butter, melted
1 cup packed dark brown sugar
1/2 cup dark corn syrup
1/2 cup light corn syrup
2 Tbsp maple syrup
1 Tbsp vanilla extract
1/2 tsp salt
2 cups pecans, toasted and chopped
1 cup pecan halves
1 phone number of a good divorce lawyer

1. The Pie Shell: Preheat oven to 425°F. Whisk the egg white and milk together. Set aside (reserve yolk for pastry). Combine flour, ground pecans, salt and sugar in the work bowl of a food processor. Add the

Chew on This

Why are pecans so darn good? Probably because they have the highest fat content of any nut— over 70%.

shortening and butter over the top and pulse a few times until the mixture has the texture of breadcrumbs. Transfer mixture to a mixing bowl.

2. Sprinkle the milk mixture gradually over the dry ingredients and mix with a wooden spoon until the dough begins to hold together. Form the dough into a disc, cover with plastic wrap and refrigerate for 30 minutes.

3. Roll dough out into a 12-inch round and transfer to a 9-inch pie pan. Trim edges to leave a 1-inch overhang and fold the edges under. Prick the bottom of the shell with a fork, brush with beaten egg yolk and cover loosely with foil. Bake in the center of the oven for 15 minutes.

4. The Filling: Beat the eggs and set aside. In a mixing bowl, combine the melted butter and brown sugar and beat until smooth. Beat in the eggs, corn syrup, maple syrup, vanilla, and salt. Fold in the chopped pecans and scrape mixture into the pie shell.

5. Carefully arrange the pecan halves over the top of the pie with a creepy, yet strangely attractive, anal-retentive intensity and bake exactly in the dead center of the preheated oven for 10 minutes. Reduce the oven temperature to 350°F and continue baking about 45 minutes until done. Cool before serving.

6. Quickly and cleverly fake your own death before someone asks you to do the dishes. Yield: One 9-inch pie

Breaker...Breaker
Banana Cream Pie

After doubling down on a double nickel across five state lines, nothing says 10-4 like a slice of truck stop-style banana cream pie.

For the Pie Crust:
1 1/2 cups chocolate wafers, finely ground
1/4 cup butter, melted
1 tsp ground cinnamon
1 Tbsp egg white, beaten

For the Filling:
3/4 cup sugar
5 Tbsp cornstarch
1/4 tsp salt
3 cups half-and-half
4 egg yolks, beaten
4 Tbsp butter
1 1/2 tsp vanilla
5 firm, ripe bananas
Juice of 1 lemon

For the Topping:
2 cups whipping cream
1/2 cup flaked coconut, toasted
1 clever and irreverent CB handle to help elevate you to
  folk-hero status
1 persistent Smokey on your tail

DID YOU KNOW?
Burt Reynolds was the top-grossing box office star from 1978–1982.

Chew on This

Trans Am, what's your pleasure? This car had its debut in 1969, and the year after *Smokey and the Bandit* was released, its popularity soared. By 1979, manufacturing was up 75 percent.

1. Make the Crust: Preheat the oven to 350°F. In a large bowl combine the ground wafers, melted butter, sugar, cinnamon and beaten egg white. Stir with a fork until evenly mixed and well moistened.

2. Empty the crust mixture into buttered 9-inch pie plate. Spread and pat mixture evenly over the sides and bottom of the pie plate and bake 10 minutes until firm.

3. Make the Filling: In a medium, heavy-bottomed saucepan sift together the sugar, cornstarch and salt. Slowly whisk in the half-and-half and the egg yolks; continue whisking until creamy and free of lumps.

4. Place over medium heat and slowly bring to a boil while whisking constantly. Reduce heat to a low simmer and continue to whisk and cook another 2 to 3 minutes until thickened. Never stop whisking.

5. Pour the hot mixture into a mixing bowl and stir in the vanilla and butter. Cover with plastic wrap and set aside to cool for 20 minutes. The plastic wrap should be placed directly on the pudding surface to prevent a skin from forming.

6. In a separate bowl, peel the bananas, slice into 1/4-inch rounds, and toss with lemon juice.

7. Fill the Pie: Pour a third of the filling into the pie crust and arrange half of the sliced bananas evenly over the filling. Spread another third of the filling over the banana layer and top with the remaining bananas. Top with the remaining filling and dust with a little toasted coconut. Refrigerate at least 1 1/2 hours or until the filling has set.

8. Top It Off: Combine the cream and the remaining coconut and whip until thickened but not stiff. Spoon coconut cream over each slice and eat rapidly.

9. Finish your coffee, tip the waitress, and hop back in your 18-wheeler. And remember, good buddy, old truckers never die, they just get a new Peterbilt™.

Yield: One 9-inch pie

May the Borscht Be with You

Spaceballs *(1987)*

A long time ago (almost as long as it's been since my ungrateful son last visited me) in a galaxy far, far away (almost as far as I'd travel for a decent bowl of borscht) . . .

2 Tbsp olive oil
6 large beets, washed and trimmed
3 large cloves garlic, peeled
1 small onion, peeled and thinly sliced
2 leeks, white part only, finely chopped
1 Granny Smith apple, peeled, cored and diced
1 small turnip, diced
2 cups chicken stock or water
Juice of 1/2 lemon
3 Tbsp rice wine vinegar
Salt and pepper to taste
1 cup sour cream
Juice and zest of 1 orange
2 Tbsp fresh dill, chopped
2 Tbsp toasted walnuts
Plenty of chutzpah
2 cinnamon rolls and some bobby pins

1. Place the beets and garlic cloves in a pot; cover with cold water and bring to a boil. Reduce the heat and simmer uncovered for 30-45 minutes, until the beets are tender.

2. While the beets cook, heat the olive oil in a large, heavy saucepan over medium-low heat. Add the sliced onion, leeks, apple and turnip. Cook slowly until tender, about 15 minutes.

3. Rinse the beets under running water until cool to the touch, the peel should slide off easily. Cut into quarters.

4. Working in batches of 2 to 3, place the beets, garlic cloves, onion

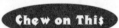

Chew on This

After the release of the *Stars Wars* prequel *Phantom Menace*, video rentals of *Spaceballs* went up a reported 73%.

mixture and the chicken stock in a blender or food processor and process until smooth. (Always use caution when blending hot food.)

5. Season with the lemon juice, rice wine vinegar, salt and pepper. Cover and chill.

6. Combine the sour cream and orange zest and set aside.

7. Ladle the soup into chilled bowls, completing each serving with a dollop of orange cream and a sprinkling of walnuts and dill.

8. So why aren't you eating? . . . Eat!
Yield: 4 servings

Food for Thought

The Beet Goes On—
Always cook beets
unpeeled with the
root attached. This
prevents flavor and
vitamins from
leeching into
the water.

INSIDE SCOOP

Director Mel Brooks is well known for his screwball comedies (*The Producers, Blazing Saddles, Young Frankenstein*) but did you know he produced the melancholy drama, *The Elephant Man*? Brooks deliberately had his name removed from the movie's publicity so people wouldn't think it was a madcap comedy.

Italian Scallion Risotto

Stayin' Alive
(1983)

One good Italian stallion deserves another. In this 1983 Sylvester Stallone-directed sequel to *Saturday Night Fever*, our hero, Tony Manero, follows his muse out of the neighborhood disco and makes the logical leap . . . *to starring on Broadway!* For our recipe, we auditioned hundreds of rice dishes but only this risotto had the right culinary choreography to make the cut. And, like Tony, it can really fill out a dance belt.

For the Vegetable Stock:
2 Tbsp olive oil
1 onion, peeled and quartered
2 carrots, coarsely chopped
2 stalks celery, coarsely chopped
15 cloves unpeeled garlic, crushed
2 cups tomatoes, coarsely chopped
1/2 bunch parsley stems
5 whole black peppercorns
1 bay leaf
2 quarts cold water

For the Risotto:
2 Tbsp butter
2 Tbsp olive oil
1/2 tsp kosher salt
1/2 cup yellow onion, finely chopped
1/2 cup dried mushrooms (morel or shiitake preferably)
2 cups Arborio rice (an Italian short-grain rice)
2 yellow squash
1/2 bunch scallions, thinly sliced on the diagonal
1 cup dry champagne
1 cup good Parmesan cheese, freshly grated
Freshly ground black pepper
1 large dance bag
1 burning desire to make it big

> **"Great dancers don't warm up. They cool down."**
> — Carlton Lesmo,
> "Dinner & a Movie"
> choreographer

Chew on This

In Northern Italy, pasta takes a back seat to rice. And the rice from the village of Arborio is most often the rice of choice. It contains a special form of starch that becomes deliciously creamy when stirred constantly while cooking.

1. **"5–6–7–8!"** . . . Combine the olive oil, onion, carrot, celery and garlic in a stockpot over medium-low heat. Cook without browning for 10 minutes, stirring, shimmying and thrusting your body forward for no real reason as often as possible.

2. Add the tomatoes, parsley stems, peppercorns and bay leaf, cover with the cold water and bring to a boil.

3. Once the stock reaches a rapid boil reduce the heat and simmer uncovered 45 minutes to an hour (longer cooking time yields a more flavored stock). Strain the stock into a saucepan, bring to a boil and reduce the liquid to no more than 4 to 5 cups. Add the dried mushrooms to the reduced stock, cover and keep hot over a very low, yet deeply intense and seething heat.

4. Combine the butter, olive oil, salt and the chopped onion in a large, thick-bottomed skillet over medium heat. Sauté the onion without browning for about 3 minutes, stirring often with a flat-edged wooden spoon or spatula until the onion is translucent.

5. Add the Arborio rice to the onion mixture and stir well to coat the rice.

6. Remove the dried mushrooms from the stock, slice thinly and set aside. Begin adding the hot vegetable stock to the rice one half cup at a time, while stirring and scraping the bottom of the pan with the wooden spoon. Allow each addition of stock to be absorbed by the rice before adding more stock. (The entire process of adding stock while stirring will take more than 20 minutes, so it may be wise to have a partner spot you in case you lose your balance or forget the routine.)

7. After 15 minutes, add the yellow squash and sliced mushrooms. Continue stirring and adding stock gradually until all of it has been absorbed by the rice, about 10 minutes. At this point, the rice should be getting tender.

8. Stir in the champagne and half of the scallions, remove from the heat and stir in the grated Parmesan. Season with a grinding of fresh black pepper and sprinkle the remaining scallions over the top. Serve at once, making sure to eat with a certain anger and intensity.

9. Celebrate your victorious risotto debut by cinching up your dance belt and executing a proud strut right out past the dirty dishes and on into the spotlight of certain culinary stardom (**Tip:** If you really want to make it big, double the recipe.)
Yield: 4 servings

INSIDE SCOOP

In addition to directing, co-producing and co-writing this film, Sylvester Stallone also supervised the rigorous physical training that transformed John Travolta from an amateur disco dancer to a buff, Broadway dancing machine. Watch for Stallone's cameo in the opening scene.

Be All That You Can Beef Stroganoff

Stripes
(1981)

Listen up, troops! The mission on which you are about to embark is not child's play. Some of you will spill stuff on your pants. And some of you, God forbid, may even mis-measure the amount of nutmeg in the sauce. But at the end of the day, you'll be able to look at yourself in the mirror and say "I'm a lean, mean cooking machine." Dismissed!

For the Beef:

2 lbs beef tenderloin, trimmed and cut into 1-inch slices

1 bay leaf, crushed

1/2 onion, thinly sliced

1/4 cup dry vermouth

Salt and pepper

For the Mushrooms and Onions:

3 Tbsp butter

3 Tbsp olive oil

1/2 lb mushrooms, quartered

3/4 cup pearl onions, peeled

For the Sauce:

2 Tbsp shallots, finely chopped

1/2 cup beef broth

1/3 cup dry vermouth

1/8 tsp nutmeg

1/4 cup heavy cream

1 cup sour cream

2 Tbsp parsley, chopped

1 shingle (optional)

> ### DID YOU KNOW?
> Screenwriter Harold Ramis penned six of the '80s' most successful comedies: *Animal House, Meatballs, Caddyshack, Ghostbusters, Back to School* and *Stripes.*

Food for Thought

Kudos to Bill Murray for finding a new use for the spatula. How many can you think of?

1. Marinate the Meat, SIR: In a large mixing bowl, combine the bay leaf, onion, and vermouth. Add beef, stir to coat, cover, and set aside for 20 minutes.

2. Sauté the Mushrooms and Onions, SIR: In a large, heavy skillet over medium-high heat, add 1 tablespoon each of the butter and olive oil. Add the mushrooms and sauté until light brown, about 3 minutes. Add the pearl onions to the pan with the mushrooms and continue sautéing 2 more minutes. Transfer the mushrooms and onions to a warm dish. Wipe the pan out, add the remaining butter and olive oil, and return to the heat.

3. Sauté the Beef, SIR: Remove the meat from the marinade and dry well with a paper towel. Season lightly with salt and pepper. Sauté in batches until nicely browned, but still rare inside. Remove the browned meat and transfer to the dish with the mushrooms and onions.

4. Make the Sauce, SIR: Add the shallots to the pan and sauté for 1 minute. Add the beef stock, vermouth, cream, nutmeg, and any juice that has collected around the mushrooms, onions, and meat. Boil and reduce the liquid until only 1/4 cup remains. Lower heat, stir in the sour cream, and bring to a low simmer. (Do not allow the sauce to come to a full boil. It will separate.)

5. Construct the Stroganoff, SIR: Fold the beef, mushrooms, and onions into the sauce and simmer for 5 minutes, until heated through.

6. Thank You, SIR, May I Have Another: Taste and adjust seasonings as desired. Serve over buttered noodles, rice, or a shingle. Garnish with chopped parsley.

7. News from the Front, SIR: Inform your dining companions that you've suddenly been called off to engage in secret nighttime training maneuvers, and will, most regrettably, be unavailable for KP duty. At ease, soldier.

Yield: 6 servings

Chew on This

MUSHROOM TIP #6

Mushrooms are tricky. When being sautéed, they initially absorb the oil in the pan. Keep cooking and watch for the oil to reappear. When it does, they're done.

Two Hot Peppers on the Lamb

**Thelma &
Louise**
(1991)

Blowing up trucks, knocking over liquor stores and running from the law can sure make you hungry. If you feel like driving off a cliff, maybe you just need a good meal . . .

For the Tomatillo Sauce:
1 lb tomatillos
4 cloves garlic, peeled
2 jalapeño peppers
1/4 cup cilantro, chopped
1/2 tsp ground cumin
1/4 tsp salt
1 cup all-purpose flour
2 eggs, beaten
Plenty of gas money and ammunition

For the Hot Peppers:
8 fresh pasilla or poblano chilies
1 lb boneless lamb loin chops
1/4 cup extra-virgin olive oil
1 tsp freshly ground black pepper
1/2 tsp oregano
1/2 lb tasty, semi-soft cheese, i.e. Gouda, Jarlsberg or
    Port-Salut, cut into little finger-sized pieces

Food for Thought

A general rule of thumb: the smaller the chili pepper the hotter it is. The ancient Aztecs used chilies as a form of torture for captured enemy warriors and adulterous wives. (A little less pepper, dear.)

Chew on This

Archeologists have found evidence of lamb's popularity at prehistoric dinner parties given as early as half a million years ago in the caves of Peking Man. But on Friday nights, did they watch "Dinner & a Cave Drawing?"

1. Too Hot to Handle: Heat an ungreased griddle or cast-iron skillet over medium-high heat. Place the tomatillos, onion and jalapeño on the griddle and roast for about 10 minutes, until the skins are blistered and dark brown.

2. Transfer mixture to a blender and add the salt, cumin and cilantro. Blend for no more than 5-10 seconds, leaving the sauce a little chunky. Transfer to a small saucepan and keep warm.

3. From the Frying Pan to the Fire: Place the peppers directly over a high flame or under the broiler, turning occasionally until the skins begin to blister and blacken on all sides. Place the roasted peppers in a paper bag and allow to sit for 15 minutes. Feel free to pass the time by taking pot shots at passing vehicles. (Big rigs with "Honk if you're Horny" bumper stickers are especially fair game.)

4. Scrape off the burnt skin under cold running water. Carefully slice a small lengthwise slit down the side of each pepper. Scrape out the seeds and pith.

5. We're On the Lamb: Trim the lamb of excess fat and cut into long thin pieces. Place the lamb strips in a small mixing bowl and toss with 2 tablespoons of the olive oil, black pepper and oregano.

6. Heat a large, heavy skillet over medium-high heat until quite hot, add a few tablespoons of olive oil and quickly add the lamb strips. Sauté until brown and crisp around the edges. (Make sure to have the exhaust fan on or a window open. If the pan is hot enough, oil tends to smoke.)

7. Stuff each pepper with a piece of cheese and a few crispy lamb strips.

8. Cut to the Chase: Wipe the skillet with a paper towel. Coat the bottom with olive oil and place over a medium-high heat. Dust each pepper with flour, dip in beaten egg and sauté until golden brown on all sides, turning as needed. (But never into Texas.)

9. For each serving, fling 2 hot peppers into a fiery pool of tomatillo sauce, garnish with a cilantro sprig and never look back.

10. Desperate Cleanup Tip: Don't. Given the choice between a) futilely tackling the towering mountain of cheese and grease encrusted dishes you're about to face and b) peacefully plummeting off an impossibly high cliff, the decision seems obvious . . . Buckle up! Yield: 4 servings

What's Under Your Skirt Steak?

Tootsie
(1982)

Only your hairdresser knows for sure . . .

2 large russet potatoes
2-3 lbs skirt steak, cut into 4 equal pieces
2 Tbsp garlic, chopped
1 tsp fresh thyme, chopped
2 tsp cracked black pepper
1 bay leaf, chopped
1 Tbsp red wine vinegar
1/2 cup olive oil
8 oz Gorgonzola cheese
2 cups leeks, thinly sliced
1 copy "An Actor Prepares"
1 jar industrial-strength bikini wax

> **"Wash your hands before and after you touch your meat."**
> —Paul Gilmartin

Chew on This

The skirt steak is actually the diaphragm muscle of the cow. It once was very inexpensive, but as it has gained popularity, its price has increased.

1. Cut the potatoes in half and cover with cold water in a saucepan. Bring to a boil, reduce the heat to a simmer and cook about 15-20 minutes.

2. The potatoes should still be firm and slightly underdone. Cool under cold running water.

3. Trim the skirt steak of excess fat and membrane, then set aside.

4. Combine the garlic, thyme, black pepper, bay leaf, vinegar and 3 tablespoons of the olive oil.

5. Rub the marinade well into the skirt steak, and then spread a thin layer of Gorgonzola onto one side of each piece.

6. Roll each piece of steak into a pinwheel and secure each with 2 small wooden skewers, one at the top and one at the bottom. (At this point it should resemble a sensible wraparound skirt.)

7. Cut each pinwheel in half at the midway point between the skewers and season with salt and pepper. Set aside.

8. Peel the potatoes and grate through the large side of a cheese grater, season with salt and pepper and set aside.

9. Heat a nonstick pan or well-seasoned cast-iron skillet with a little olive oil. When it is quite hot, spoon in about 1 cup of grated potato and a small handful of sliced leeks and spread to cover bottom of pan. Cover the leeks with another half-cup of potato and sauté over medium heat until crisp and light brown. Flip and brown the other side, then transfer to a cookie sheet and keep warm.

10. Wipe the hot pan with a paper towel to remove any remaining potato. Increase the heat to medium-high and open the windows. (It might get a little smoky.)

11. Sear the skirt steak about 2-3 minutes on each side for medium-rare, 4-5 minutes for medium, 6-7 minutes for well done, and 12-14 hours for jerky.

12. Serve each steak on a potato bed, peel off your lashes, pull off your falsies, sit down, and eat like a man.
Yield: 4 servings

Food for Thought

Dustin Hoffman had a clause in his *Tootsie* contract guaranteeing him the right to pull out of the picture if he didn't like his character's make-up.

INSIDE SCOOP

In addition to his Best Actor Oscar® nomination for this film, Dustin Hoffman has been nominated six other times. He has won twice, once for *Kramer vs. Kramer* and again for *Rain Man.*

Celery (Root of All Evil) Soup with Pork Belly Croutons

Trading Places
(1983)

Dan Aykroyd and Eddie Murphy live out a nature vs. nurture experiment in this 1983 comedy classic. We contend that all good things come not just from nature or nurture, but from a combination of the two. Celery root, for instance, was created by nature, but with a little nurturing can be made into this delicious soup.

For the Vegetable Stock:
2 Tbsp olive oil
2 leeks, thinly sliced
5 cloves unpeeled garlic, crushed
1 1/2 tsp salt
2 stalks celery, chopped
1 fennel bulb, sliced
1/2 bunch parsley stems
5 whole black peppercorns
1 bay leaf
1/2 cup white wine
1 1/2 quarts cold water

For the Soup:
1 large celery root (also called celeriac), peeled and diced
1 medium yellow potato, peeled and sliced
1 medium yellow onion, thinly sliced
1 medium leek, thinly sliced
1 sprig each: thyme and tarragon, tied together with a piece of string
1/2 cup cream
1/2 lb pork belly (bacon), diced
2 cups French bread, cubed
An uncanny, innate sense of global commodities

1. Combine the olive oil, leeks, garlic and salt in a stock pot over medium-low heat. Cook slowly without browning for 10 minutes.

Food for Thought

Celery root and common celery are different varieties of the same plant, one grown for its crunchy stalk, the other for the root. Until the 17th century, both types were among those infamous foods thought by gastronomes to be powerful aphrodisiacs and were used solely for medicinal purposes.

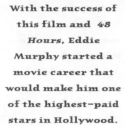

Chew on This

With the success of this film and *48 Hours*, Eddie Murphy started a movie career that would make him one of the highest-paid stars in Hollywood.

2. Add the celery, fennel, parsley stems, peppercorns, bay leaf and white wine; cook until the wine reduces by half, add the cold water and bring to a boil.

3. Reduce the heat and simmer uncovered anywhere from 30-45 minutes (a longer cooking time generally yields a more highly flavorful stock, but there is no penalty for early withdrawal).

4. Strain the stock into a large saucepan. (You may skip steps 1–4 if using a canned stock . . . not as rich but a recommended stock option nonetheless.)

5. Combine the celery root, leek, onion, potato and the bundled herb sprigs with the stock.

6. Cover and simmer until the vegetables are soft, about 30 minutes.

7. Meanwhile, call your broker. If pork bellies are up, proceed to the next step, if pork bellies are down, consider diversifying your ingredients and attempting this recipe during the next fiscal year.

8. Fry pork belly until crisp; drain all but one tablespoon of fat from the pan and stir in bread cubes. Cook, stirring often until golden brown. Set aside.

9. Remove the bundled herbs from the soup; puree mixture in a food processor or blender.

10. Stir in the cream; check and correct seasonings to taste. Cover and keep warm.

11. Call your guests to the table. If their interest remains at an all time high, divide soup into four bowls, garnish with pork belly croutons and ask yourself again: "How can anything so inherently evil taste so good?"
Yield: 4 servings

INSIDE SCOOP

Apparently, piggish behavior is nothing new to the New York Stock Market. History tells us that founding city fathers were having so much trouble with marauding hogs that they built a long wall across town. Today we know it as Wall Street. (Maybe the wall should go back up?)

Mussels and Shrimp

Arnold Schwarzenegger and Danny DeVito play improbable twins in this 1988 comedy about genetic engineering's efforts to create the perfect man. In the "Dinner & a Movie" test kitchen, we've used culinary engineering to create the perfect recipe, Mussels & Shrimp.

2 lbs large shrimp
2 lbs mussels
1 cup dry white wine
1/4 tsp saffron threads
1/2 cup olive oil
2 bell peppers, diced
1 onion, diced
2 Tbsp garlic, chopped
1 cup artichoke hearts, quartered
1 bay leaf
1 tsp paprika
4 cups chicken stock
1 1/2 cups canned plum tomatoes, chopped
2 cups Arborio rice or short-grain rice
1/2 cup frozen tiny peas
1 cup Spanish olives, sliced
1 ranch fresh egg, divided in two (1/2 beaten, the other half coddled)

1. Peel and devein shrimp, clean and scrub mussels.

2. In a small saucepan, bring wine to a boil, add the saffron and remove from heat.

3. Heat olive oil over medium heat in the largest, heaviest skillet or saucepan you've got. Add the peppers and onion until the onion softens, about 3 minutes.

4. Add the garlic, artichokes, bay leaf and paprika and sauté a minute more. Add the rice and stir to coat.

5. Add chicken stock and tomatoes, increase heat and bring to a boil. Reduce heat to medium and cook uncovered for about 15 minutes.

Chew on This

The six-foot-two-inch Arnold Schwarzenegger is called by the *Guinness Book of World Records,* "the most perfectly developed man in the history of the world." During his career, he has won over twenty body-building titles and was named Mr. Universe four times and Mr. Olympia seven times.

6. Add the saffron-infused wine, shrimp and mussels, cover and continue cooking about 15 minutes until the rice is tender and the mussels pop open.

7. Season to taste with salt and pepper. Five minutes before serving, mix in the green peas and olives.

8. Be sure to save room for some "Separated at Birthday Cake." Yield: 4 servings

INSIDE SCOOP

The five-foot-tall Danny DeVito was once a hairdresser, whose clients affectionately called him "Mr. Danny." DeVito's career has been anything but diminutive. His production company, Jersey Films, has produced such stylish movies as *Pulp Fiction* and *Out of Sight*.

Food for Thought

We think the maxim about shellfish being safe in any month with the letter "R" should be put to rest. "Red Tides" can and do occur all throughout the year, creating hot spots where shellfish are indeed unsafe to eat. When purchasing shellfish it's best to shop in a reputable store, one that buys fish from a licensed USDA-inspected vendor. If digging for shellfish yourself, use that big muscle between your ears and check with the health department for a local shellfish update.

"No Bull" Tequila Fajitas

Urban Cowboy

(1980)

Originally, this recipe called for a mechanical bull, but, not surprisingly, our butcher got electrocuted when he tried to bone out the loin. We use only chicken and shrimp in this mouthwatering, "bull-free" creation:

For the Marinade:
3 Roma tomatoes, cut in quarters
1/2 cup cilantro, coarsely chopped
1/2 yellow onion, coarsely chopped
8 cloves garlic, peeled
1/2 cup beer (ah, leftovers you can love)
1/4 cup tequila
1/4 cup lime juice
3 Tbsp olive oil
2 tsp canned chipotle pepper

For the No Bull Fajitas:
1 lb skinless, boneless
  chicken breasts
1 lb tiger shrimp
1 red onion, thinly sliced
2 pasilla peppers, seeded
  and thinly sliced
8-12 flour tortillas

For the Salsa:
1 lb tomatillos,
  husks removed
4 cloves garlic, peeled
2 serrano peppers,
  peeled and seeded
1/2 cup cilantro, chopped
1/2 tsp ground cumin
1/4 tsp salt

For the Garnishes:
3 ripe Roma tomatoes, diced
1 avocado, peeled, pitted and sliced
1 cup sour cream
1 4-oz can pickled jalapeños
1/2 cup Jack cheese or dry Mexican cheese, crumbled
1 cup shredded red cabbage
1 tsp oregano
1 "Don't Mess with Texas" T-shirt
1 subscription to *Mobile Home & Garden*

1. Move #1: Place all ingredients for the marinade in a food processor or blender and blend until smooth. Peel and devein the shrimp. Cut the

Chew on This

After defining the disco era with Saturday Night Fever, *Travolta went on to set a new era's musical style with this movie and its bestselling soundtrack. Critics still refer to the country music of the 1980s as the "Urban Cowboy" period.*

chicken breast into strips. Place shrimp and chicken in separate nonreactive bowls, and add half of the marinade to each. Cover and refrigerate.

2. Move #2: Heat a griddle or cast-iron skillet over medium-high heat. Place the tomatillos, garlic, and serranos on the griddle and roast for about 10 minutes until the skins are blistered and dark brown. Transfer to a blender or food processor and blend for no more than 10 seconds. Transfer to a bowl and stir in the cilantro, cumin, and salt. Set aside for flavors to blend.

3. Time to Really Move It, Pardner: Clean and reheat the griddle over high heat. While the griddle is heating up, open a couple of Lone Stars™ and clean up the trailer. Shred the cabbage and toss with oregano and a little juice from the pickled jalapeños. Warm the tortillas.

4. When the griddle is hot, grab a handful each of the chicken and the shrimp, squeeze out excess marinade and toss onto the griddle along with some red onion and pasilla pepper. If the griddle is hot enough, you're in for about a 2-minute ride.

5. Move It Out: Wrap meat in warmed tortillas; add sauce and garnishes to each plate. Hold on tight and don't let go.
Yield: 4 servings

> **"Pork tastes good.**
> **Bacon tastes good."**
> —John Travolta as Vincent Vega
> in *Pulp Fiction*

Food for Thought

In the old days of cattle ranching, when Texas ranchers butchered a cow, they would keep the best meat and give the scraps to their ranch hands. These "vaqueros" would grill the meat over the fire, slice it and wrap it in tortillas. The fajita was born. It wasn't until the late 1960s, though, that Sonny "Fajita King" Falcon began selling fajitas at events throughout Texas, bringing this Tex-Mex delicacy to a wider audience.

Ice-Cold War Martinis and Secret Spy Snacks

This 1985 Bond film gives Roger Moore barely enough time to eat. Luckily these Cold War snacks can be assembled quickly, eaten on the run, and chased down with the quintessential Bond dry martini.

For the Ice-Cold Martinis:
Cracked ice
12 oz vodka
1 1/2 oz dry vermouth
1 lemon

For the Lemon Cream:
1/2 cup whipping cream
1/2 cup sour cream
2 tsp lemon juice

For the Parmesan Twists:
1 sheet frozen puff pastry
1 egg, beaten with 1 Tbsp milk
1/2 cup grated Parmesan cheese
1 tsp sesame seeds

For the Secret Spy Snacks:
4 small red potatoes, cooked and chilled
1 English cucumber
12 cherry tomatoes
2 oz smoked salmon
2 oz smoked chicken
2 oz Beluga caviar
1 bunch fresh dill
1 tuxedo
1 license to kill (or learner's permit, if accompanied by a licensed killer over 18)

THINGS YOU WOULD NEVER HEAR JAMES BOND SAY

1 "Stirred, not shaken."

2 "Can't you just hold me? I'd rather just cuddle."

3 "Do I look fat in these pants?"

1. Have an Ice-Cold War Martini: Fill a mixing glass with cracked ice. Measure in the vodka and vermouth. Shake, do not stir. Strain into iced glasses.

2. Make the Lemon Twists: Cut two thin strips of lemon peel. Release their essential oils by firmly twisting. Rub lemon twists around the rims of the glasses before depositing dead center in each glass and offering a toast to Her Majesty, the Queen.

3. Make the Lemon Cream: Whip the cream until soft peaks form. Fold in the sour cream and lemon juice; cover and refrigerate 20 minutes.

4. Make the Parmesan Twists: Preheat oven to 400°F. Lay out puff pastry and brush with the egg mixture. Sprinkle with the Parmesan and sesame seeds. Cut the sheet into 1/2-inch-wide strips and twist a few times. Bake for 10-15 minutes, until golden.

5. Prepare the Secret Spy Snacks: Slice the potatoes and cucumber into rounds 1/2-inch thick. Using a melon baller or small spoon, scoop out a shallow indentation in the center of each slice, being careful not to go all the way through.

6. Remove the stems from the cherry tomatoes, cut tops off tomatoes, scoop out the seeds and pulp with a small spoon.

7. Fill the prepared potato, cucumber, and tomato bases with smoked fish, smoked chicken, or caviar. Top with cold lemon cream and garnish with a small sprig of dill.

8. Serve with the Parmesan twists and a second round of martinis.

9. Play the Secret Agent Party Game! Announce that you've frozen some politically explosive microfilm in one of the ice cubes. Whoever finds it must pummel the largest guest, seduce the hostess and escape without using the door or helping with the dishes. (Hey, the Cold War may be over, but that doesn't mean the fun has to come to an end.)
Yield: 4 servings

INSIDE SCOOP
A *View to a Kill* is Roger Moore's last appearance as 007.

Nuclear Subs with Dressing of the Former Soviet Union

War Games
(1983)

Be a hero in your own kitchen! Like our young David Lightman and the W.O.P.R., try programming your microwave to understand the futility of culinary thermonuclear confrontation (always embarrassing when guests are over). Modern household appliances should always be used for good, never evil.

Russian Dressing:
4 Tbsp sun dried tomatoes, pureed or finely minced
1/2 cup mayonnaise
2 tsp lemon juice
1 green onion

Olive Tapenade:
1 cup oil-cured black olives, pitted
1/4 tsp red pepper flakes
1-2 cloves garlic, minced
2 Tbsp capers
1 fresh thyme sprig, coarsely chopped
1/8 cup extra-virgin olive oil

The Sub:
2 half chicken breasts, skinned and boned
1 Tbsp olive oil
2 sprigs fresh rosemary
1/2 cup water
2 yellow bell peppers
1/4 lb prosciutto, thinly sliced
1/4 lb provolone, thinly sliced
1 (war) head butter lettuce
2 loaves baguette-style French bread
1 bowl microchips, well salted

1. Shall We Play a Game?: Combine all dressing ingredients, mix well, cover, and refrigerate.

Chew on This

Russian dressing was invented in 1940 at Delmonico's restaurant in New York City.

2. Prepare the Tapenade: If using a food processor, combine all tapenade ingredients, and process the mixture briefly (2 or 3 pulses). If chopping by hand, combine olives, garlic, and capers on a board and chop together coarsely. Transfer to a bowl, add thyme and olive oil, mix with a wooden spoon.

3. Cook the Chicken Breasts: Season chicken breasts with salt and pepper. In a small sauté pan heat olive oil over medium-high heat. Place the chicken in the pan smooth-side down and sauté for 2-3 minutes, until nicely browned. Reduce heat to medium-low and turn the breasts over. Place a rosemary sprig on each breast, add the water, and cover. Continue cooking for another 10 minutes, or until the meat is firm to the touch. Remove pan from heat and let chicken cool in the broth. When cool enough to handle, slice chicken on the diagonal as thinly as possible and set aside.

4. Roast the Peppers: Preheat broiler. Rub whole peppers lightly with a tiny bit of olive oil and place under the broiler as close to the heat as possible. Using long tongs, turn every minute until the skin on all sides is black and blistered. Transfer the peppers to a paper bag, close the top, and let cool for 5 minutes. Remove peppers and, while holding them under running water, peel the burnt skin off. Remove the seeds and white membrane. Dry the peppers, cut lengthwise into 1-inch strips, and set aside.

5. Construct the Sandwiches: Cut the baguettes in half lengthwise. Spread the olive tapenade on the bottom half and the dressing of the former Soviet Union on the top half. Building from bottom to top, construct your sub with chicken, peppers, prosciutto, provolone, tomatoes, and lettuce and the top piece of bread. Cut each baguette in 4-6 pieces.

Yield: 4-6 servings

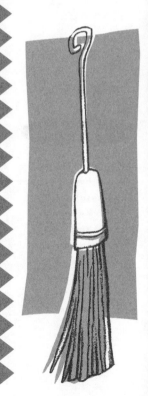

INSIDE SCOOP

Credit for the creation of the first "sandwich" is customarily given to an Englishman named John Montague, aka. the Earl of Sandwich.

> Just think, had we launched this sub in the spirit of gastronomic glasnost, neither of our countries would have gone flat broke.
>
> MAKE SNACKS NOT WAR

Mouthwatering Kathleen Turnovers

Can you blame us? "Mouth Watering Michael Douglases" just didn't sound as good.

For the Pastry:
1 1/2 cups all-purpose flour, sifted
1 cup cake flour, sifted
1/4 tsp salt
1 tsp sugar
6 Tbsp vegetable shortening, chilled
1/2 cup butter, chilled and cut into small pieces
1/3 cup cream cheese, softened
1-2 Tbsp ice water, as needed
1 egg, beaten (for egg wash)

For the Spinach Filling:
1/2 lb frozen spinach
2 scallions, chopped
1/4 cup fresh parsley, chopped
1/4 cup fresh dill, chopped
1/2 cup walnut pieces
3 Tbsp olive oil
1/2 onion, peeled and diced
1 cup feta cheese, crumbled
1/4 cup cottage cheese
1 egg
Pinch nutmeg

For the Apple Filling:
2 baking apples, peeled, cored and thinly sliced
1 tsp lemon juice
1/4 cup golden raisins
1/2 cup cranberry juice
1/2 tsp ground cinnamon
1/4 cup powdered sugar
1 Tbsp butter
A good divorce attorney

Chew on This

Director Danny Devito had to fight to maintain the dark ending of this film. Not surprisingly, the studio wanted to change it to something happier.

1. Make the Pie Crust: In a medium bowl, mix together the flours, salt and sugar. Using a pastry blender (or two knives), work the shortening into the flour until it resembles coarse cornmeal. Add butter and continue cutting until mixture resembles small peas. Add the cream cheese one tablespoon at a time, mixing with a fork after each addition. If the dough feels dry, add ice water, a few drops at a time. Using your hands, gently shape the dough into a disc. Wrap with plastic wrap and refrigerate for 20 minutes.

2. Make the Spinach Filling: Squeeze excess water from the spinach and toss with the scallions, parsley, dill and walnuts in a large mixing bowl.

3. Heat the olive oil in a large skillet over medium heat, add the onion and sauté until translucent, about 5 minutes. Stir in the spinach mixture and remove from heat to cool.

4. Mix together the cheeses, egg and nutmeg in a small mixing bowl. Stir the cheese mixture into the spinach mixture, check seasonings and set aside.

5. Make the Apple Filling: Combine the apples, lemon juice, raisins, cranberry juice, cinnamon, powdered sugar and butter. Bring to a boil, reduce heat and simmer for 10-15 minutes until thickened. Remove from heat and set aside to cool.

6. Make the Spinach Turnovers: Line 2 large baking sheets with parchment paper and preheat the oven to 400°F.

7. Cut the dough into two equal pieces; wrap and return one piece to the refrigerator. Dust a clean work surface with flour and roll the dough out into a rectangle measuring approximately 12x16 inches. Trim any ragged edges and divide dough into 4 even pieces.

8. Spoon 4 to 5 tablespoons of filling onto each rectangle, brush the edges with egg wash and fold over to enclose the filling. Crimp the sealed edges gently with the tines of a fork and brush the tops with egg wash. Transfer the turnovers to a prepared baking sheet.

9. Make the Apple Turnovers: Roll out the remaining dough to a thickness of about 1/8 inch (a little thicker than a quarter). Use a 5-or 6-inch round cutter to cut out 4 rounds. Fill each with 1/4 cup of apple filling. Egg wash the inside edges, fold over and seal as with the spinach turnovers.

10. Brush the top of each turnover with eggwash and dust with a little sugar; transfer to baking sheet with spinach turnovers and bake 20 minutes, until golden.

11. Before diving into the snacks, have each guest sign a prenuptial agreement forfeiting all rights to leftovers.
Yield: 8 turnovers

Food for Thought

The possibilities are endless. Whether steamed, baked or fried, filled with truffles, curry, apricots or fried pork, the ubiquitous and flexible turnover makes gratifying appearances throughout the world.

INSIDE SCOOP

Long-time collaborators Danny DeVito and Michael Douglas were roommates when they were starting out as actors.

Baby Steppin' Kabobs

What About Bob?
(1991)

This therapeutic comedy, starring Bill Murray as a man paralyzed by fear, is close to our hearts here at "Dinner & a Movie." We know a lot of you out there are watching on Friday nights but you're still afraid to cook along. Don't be afraid, as you'll see in this recipe, it all starts with one little step . . .

1-2 lbs loin cut beef, lamb or pork
1 1/2 Tbsp garlic, peeled and minced
1 Tbsp tomato paste
3 Tbsp freshly squeezed lemon juice
1 Tbsp soy sauce
2-3 tsp fresh rosemary, summer savory, thyme or
   parsley, chopped
1/4 cup extra-virgin olive oil
Black pepper, cayenne and cumin to taste
1 lb small red potatoes
12 small boiling onions
1 pint cherry tomatoes
15 small mushrooms
2 bell peppers, cut into quarters
2 small yellow squash or zucchini cut into 1-2-inch slices
Any other seasonal and skewerable veggies you come across
   at the market.
Wooden or metal skewers
1 copy of Claud Mann's runaway bestseller, *Take a Whisk!*

Baby Step 1. Put first-aid kit out where you can get to it in a hurry.

Baby Step 2. Take a deep breath. Go to the store and buy the stuff. (Remember to use hanky when touching door handles, money or people.)

Baby Step 3. Trim the meat of as much fat as possible and cut into thin slices. Wash hands.

Baby Step 4. Combine all marinade ingredients in a mixing bowl and pour half over the meat. Mix well to coat evenly. (Remember to breathe.) Smell fingers.

Chew on This

The words *shish kebab* are derived from a pair of Turkish words that mean "skewer" and "roast meat."

Baby Step 5. In a medium saucepan, combine the potatoes, onions and 1 teaspoon of salt. Cover with cold water and bring to a boil.

Baby Step 6. Reduce heat and simmer 10 minutes. Drain potatoes and onions, rinse with cool water and set aside. Rinse hands.

Baby Step 7. Thread the meat securely onto the skewers. If using wooden skewers, soak them in water a few minutes before skewering. Wash hands twice.

Baby Step 8. Step by step, fearlessly skewer the vegetable one by one until your skewer is full. Once that skewer fills up, repeat the process until you either run out of skewers or veggies. Don't feel bad when you run out, you're supposed to. Brush veggie skewers with marinade then think about washing hands.

Baby Step 9. Warn fire department, then light barbecue. Check to see if eyebrows remain, if so, go on to next step.

Baby Step 10. Quietly repeat over and over, "This time, my skewers will hold together and not catch fire."

Baby Step 11. Cook veggie skewers about 5-6 minutes, turning once or twice. Transfer to warm platter. Pat self on back. Don't even think about washing hands.

Baby Step 12. Cook the meat skewers 3-4 minutes, close to the flame, turning once. Breathe in the victorious aroma of smoky conquest . . . crisp and succulent. Eat, dance, rejoice.

Baby Step 13. Celebrate breakthrough by boldly leaving the dishes piled high and dirty in the sink like a proud and defiant monument to your bravery.

Baby Step 14. Call shrink and cancel next appointment. (Confirm the following appointment, just in case.)
Yield: 4 servings

FOOD THERAPY

Food still got you frightened? Here are some other titles from the "Dinner & a Movie" culinary Self-help Library:

— *Your Inner Julia Child*

— *I'm C-O-O.K. You're C-O-O.K.*

— *Simmering Abundance*

— *Road to Salivation*

— *Chop Wood Carry Parsley*

— *Be Hare Now*

INSIDE SCOOP

After some early hard knocks, Bill Murray took a baby step toward changing his life by joining his older brother Brian in the cast of Chicago's Second City comedy troupe. Murray went on to star in the "National Lampoon Radio Hour" and eventually was tapped to replace Chevy Chase on "Saturday Night Live."

Know Your Terms!

Beat 1) to vigorously stir to blend ingredients. 2) the pregnant pauses between the important lines an actor has and the stuff the other actors say.

Beefcake 1) pastry-encased meat of a bovine animal. 2) well-muscled actor who finds himself shirtless more often than not.

Blanch 1) to cook briefly in a liquid. 2) best-known Tennessee Williams character, who claimed to depend on the kindness of strangers. (This *Blanche* has an "e" at the end.)

Blend 1) to combine and mix ingredients well. 2) what an extra actor does if he wants to keep working.

Butterfly 1) to split open and spread apart. 2) something that forms in actors' stomachs prior to their walking on stage and forgetting their lines.

Caper 1) the pickled bud of the caper bush. 2) popular genre of action-adventure movie.

Chafing 1) a type of dish used to keep food hot at the table. 2) painful condition suffered by many actors working in westerns.

Cheesy 1) dish using cheese as a key ingredient. 2) movie containing an over-abundance of saccharine moments.

Coddle 1) to gently cook in very hot, but not boiling, water. 2) how a star actor is treated regardless of his behavior.

Corny 1) dish employing large amounts of corn. 2) much like Cheesy, but less believable.

Cottage Cheese 1) a fresh, unripened cheese. 2) good reason for use of a body double.

Curdling 1) denaturing process caused by enzymes, acidity, or heat whereby milk separates and turns to curd. 2) type of spine-tingling, high-pitched scream employed by actresses in horror movies.

Cut 1) to divide into pieces with the use of a sharp knife. 2) what the director shouts to stop the cameras from rolling.

Demi-Glace 1) a very highly reduced meat stock. 2) lipstick specifically formulated to be used under bright lights.

Dice 1) to cut food into small uniform cubes. 2) clever middle name of former stand-up comedian turned actor (see also Hack).

Emulsion 1) a mixture composed of a suspension of fat globules. 2) light-sensitive coating on movie film that causes it to capture and retain an image.

Flake 1) to break apart into small pieces. 2) to forget to show up for rehearsal.

Fold 1) to combine ingredients with a gentle, circular motion. 2) what generally happens to a show after unanimously scathing reviews.

Fool 1) English dessert consisting of fruit folded into whipping cream or custard. 2) word most used by stockholders when describing the studio executive who passed on *E.T.*

Gel 1) to congeal with the use of gelatin or pectin. 2) color filter used over stage lighting.

Ginger 1) aromatic rhizome commonly used in Asian cooking. 2a) the one you chose over Mary Ann. 2b) the one you chose over Cyd Charisse.

Glaze 1) to brush a dish with a light coating of sauce. 2a) look commonly seen in the eyes of Hollywood agents when discussing large amounts of money. 2b) official doughnut of the teamster's union, Hollywood local.

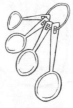

Grate 1) to cut food into small bits with the use of a grater. 2) the effect that actors crossing over into singing careers have on the ears of the hearing.

Grease 1) to wipe fat onto a pan to keep food from sticking to it. 2) incredibly popular musical starring middle-aged teenaged actors.

Grind 1) to reduce a food into powder by crushing between hard surfaces. 2) how a $300,000-a-week television actor describes his job after a grueling two seasons.

Hack 1) to forcefully cut with uneven or irregular blows. 2) an actor who's either been in more than one infomercial, or should be.

Ham 1) the cured thigh or hind leg from a hog or pig. 2) actor who can't differentiate on-stage from off-stage.

Junket 1) a rennet-thickened, milk-based dessert. 2) an all-expenses-paid vacation for the Hollywood press corps in which they're allowed to follow a star around and ask probing and insightful questions.

Loins 1) the tender cuts of meat taken from the front quarter of an animal on either side of the backbone. 2) common spot for aching to be felt by characters in the "coming of age" film genre.

Mace 1) popular baking spice found in the outer layer of the fruit of the nutmeg tree. 2) popular defensive aerosol used by actresses to keep frisky paparazzi at bay.

Mint 1) any of several aromatic herbs belonging to the mint family. 2) cost of an average Kevin Costner spectacle.

Mole 1) famous Mexican sauce containing, among other things, chilies, chocolate, garlic, and sesame seeds. 2) trademark facial imperfection.

Mousse 1) dish consisting of a flavoring base folded into whipped cream or egg whites. 2) gooey hair product very popular with moody young actors appearing in John Hughes movies.

Pasties 1) little meat-and-vegetable turnovers. 2) the difference between an "R" or an "NC17" rating.

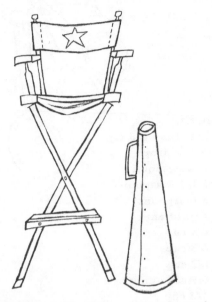

Pearl Barley 1) a highly polished form of barley commonly used in soup. 2) highly polished singer commonly seen in old movies.

Roll 1) a small, rounded individual portion of bread. 2) what the director shouts to begin filming.

Saccharin 1) non-caloric sugar substitute approximately 500 times sweeter than sugar. 2) a shameless display of insincere emotion.

Score 1) to partially cut through the outer surface of a food. 2) musical composition that, when recorded, becomes part of the soundtrack of a film.

Season 1) enhance the taste of food through the use of spices, herbs, etc. 2) a recurrent or specific division of time marked by new film and television releases.

Shark 1) family of edible predatory fish growing up to forty feet in length. 2) See "Agent" below.

Shot 1) one jigger full of alcoholic spirits. 2) one in a series of camera angles.

Spit 1) metal rod used to skewer and cook food over an open flame. 2) foamy liquid often found issuing forth from the mouths of emotionally charged actors.

Skin 1) to remove the external membranous tissue from a piece of fish or poultry. 2) the weaker the script, the more of this you're likely to see.

Thickening Agent 1) any of various ingredients used to thicken sauces, soups, etc. 2) an actor's representative after too many power lunches.

Standard Abbreviations

teaspoon	t / tsp
tablespoon	T / TBL / Tbsp
TBS	the superstation!
Cup	c
Quart	qt
Pound	lb
Ounce	oz

Standard Measurement Equivalents

A few grains/pinch/dash, etc. (dry)	=	Less than 1/8 tsp
A dash (liquid)	=	A few drops
3 teaspoons	=	1 tablespoon
1/2 tablespoon	=	1-1/2 teaspoons
1 tablespoon	=	3 teaspoons
2 tablespoons	=	1 fluid ounce
4 tablespoons	=	1/4 cup
5-1/3 tablespoons	=	1/3 cup
8 tablespoons	=	1/2 cup
8 tablespoons	=	4 fluid ounces
10-2/3 tablespoons	=	2/3 cup
12 tablespoons	=	3/4 cup
16 tablespoons	=	1 cup
16 tablespoons	=	8 fluid ounces
1/8 cup	=	2 tablespoons
1/4 cup	=	4 tablespoons
1/4 cup	=	2 fluid ounces
1/3 cup	=	5 tablespoons plus 1 teaspoon
1/2 cup	=	8 tablespoons
1 cup	=	16 tablespoons
1 cup	=	8 fluid ounces
1 cup	=	1/2 pint
2 cups	=	1 pint
2 pints	=	1 quart
4 quarts (liquid)	=	1 gallon
8 quarts (dry)	=	1 peck
4 pecks (dry)	=	1 bushel
1 kilogram	=	approximately 2 pounds
1 liter	=	approximately 4 cups or 1 quart

Approximate Metric Equivalents by Volume

U.S.	METRIC		METRIC	U.S.
1/4 cup	60 milliliters		50 milliliters	.21 cup
1/2 cup	120 milliliters		100 milliliters	.42 cup
1 cup	230 milliliters		150 milliliters	.63 cup
1 1/4 cups	300 milliliters		200 milliliters	.84 cup
1 1/2 cups	360 milliliters		250 milliliters	1.06 cups
2 cups	460 milliliters		1 liter	1.05 quarts
2 1/2 cups	600 milliliters			
3 cups	700 milliliters			
4 cups (1 quart)	.95 liter			
1.06 quarts	1 liter			
4 quarts (1 gallon)	3.8 liters			

Approximate Metric Equivalents by Weight

U.S.	METRIC		METRIC	U.S.
1/4 ounce	7 grams		1 gram	.035 ounce
1/2 ounce	14 grams		50 grams	1.75 ounces
1 ounce	28 grams		100 grams	3.5 ounces
1 1/4 ounces	35 grams		250 grams	8.75 ounces
1 1/2 ounces	40 grams		500 grams	1.1 pounds
2 1/2 ounces	70 grams		1 kilogram	2.2 pounds
4 ounces	112 grams			
5 ounces	140 grams			
8 ounces	228 grams			
10 ounces	280 grams			
15 ounces	425 grams			
16 ounces (1 pound)	454 grams			

Temperature Conversions

To convert from Fahrenheit to Celsius: subtract 32, multiply by 5, divide by 9.
To convert from Celsius to Fahrenheit: multiply by 9, divide by 5, add 32.

250 degrees F	**= 120 degrees C**
275 degrees F	**= 140 degrees C**
300 degrees F	**= 150 degrees C**
325 degrees F	**= 160 degrees C**
350 degrees F	**= 180 degrees C**
375 degrees F	**= 190 degrees C**
400 degrees F	**= 200 degrees C**
425 degrees F	**= 220 degrees C**
450 degrees F	**= 230 degrees C**
475 degrees F	**= 240 degrees C**
500 degrees F	**= 260 degrees C**

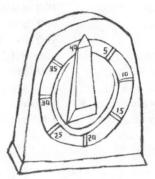

Boiling point of water at various altitudes.

	Degrees F	Degrees C
Sea Level	212°	100°
2,000 ft.	208°	98°
5,000 ft.	203°	95°
7,500 ft.	198°	92°
10,000 ft.	194°	90°

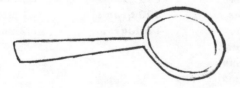

Unsifted Flour

1 tbs	1/4 ounce
1/4 cup	1 1/4 ounces
1/2 cup	2 1/2 ounces
2/3 cup	3 1/4 ounces
3/4 cup	3 1/2 ounces
1 cup	5 ounces

Granulated Sugar

1 tsp	1/6 ounce
1 Tbsp	1/2 ounce
1/4 cup	1 3/4 ounces
1/3 cup	2 1/4 ounces
1/2 cup	3 1/2 ounces
2/3 cup	4 1/2 ounces
1 cup	7 ounces

Butter and Shortening

1 Tbsp	1/8 stick	1/2 ounce
2 Tbsp	1/4 stick	1 ounce
4 Tbsp	1/2 stick	2 ounces
8 Tbsp (1 stick)	4 ounces	1/4 lb

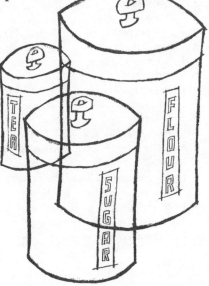

Bare Bones Essential Equipment

Just have a can opener and a hotplate, but can't quite put your finger on what's missing?
Here's a great list to help get you started:

- One 8-10" high carbon, stainless steel chef's knife *(sometimes called a French knife)*
- One 4" paring knife
- One 6-8" utility knife
- 18-10" serrated knife
- 1 oyster knife
- One sharpening steel
- At least 2 vegetable peelers *(we usually lose one)*
- 1 pair kitchen shears
- 1 corkscrew
- 1 bottle opener
- 1 cheese grater
- 1 can opener
- 1 pepper mill
- 3 cutting boards *(one all-purpose, one for pastry and one small one just for garlic, onion, chilies, etc.)*
- 2 glass measuring cups *(one 1-cup, one 2-cup)*
- 1 set dry measuring cups
- 1 set measuring spoons
- 1 oven thermometer
- 1 instant-read meat thermometer
- 3 nested stainless mixing bowls
- 3 nested glass mixing bowls
- 1 rubber spatula
- 1 pancake-type turner
- 2 or 3 wooden spoons
- 1 large slotted spoon
- 1 large metal spoon
- 1 fine mesh skimmer
- 1 medium mesh strainer
- 1 colander
- 1 funnel
- 1 pastry brush
- 1 ladle

- 1 pair tongs
- 1 large 2-3 tine fork
- 1 balloon whisk
- 1 rotary beater
- 1 rolling pin
- 10 "Dinner & a Movie" Cookbooks
- 1 kitchen timer
- 1 2 qt. saucepan with cover
- 1 3 qt. saucepan with cover
- 1 steamer basket
- 1 Dutch oven with cover
- 1 10-12 qt. stockpot with cover
- 1 8" sauté pan with cover
- 1 10" sauté pan with cover
- 1 12" cast-iron skillet with cover
- 1 8-10" nonstick omelet pan
- 1 roasting pan
- 1 roasting rack
- 1 flat cookie sheet
- 1 glass pie plate
- 1 2 qt. glass casserole
- 1 aluminum loaf pan
- 1 muffin tin
- 1 fire extinguisher
- 1 salad spinner
- 1 tea kettle
- 1 blender *(with or without goldfish)*
- 1 remote control *(which conveniently defaults to TBS)*
- 1 programmable VCR and lots of blank tapes *(in case you miss "Dinner & a Movie")*
- 1 TV scheduling guide *(to find out if "Dinner & a Movie" is on before or after the Braves)*
- 1 charming co-host of choice

Goods to Keep on Hand

Wonder what to keep in your larder? To be honest, we're not quite sure what a larder is, but if we had one, these are some of the things we'd keep in it:

DRY GOODS

all-purpose flour
baking chocolate
baking powder
baking soda
brown rice
brown sugar
cake flour
cocoa powder
corn meal
corn starch
dried beans
dried pasta
dry active yeast
granulated sugar
kosher salt
shelled nuts, i.e. walnuts, almonds, pecans, peanuts
table salt or sea salt
white rice

CANNED AND BOTTLED

anchovies
balsamic vinegar
canned beef stock
capers
canned chicken stock
Dijon mustard
extra-virgin olive oil
honey
hot pepper sauce
ketchup
mayonnaise
pure maple syrup
pure olive oil
pure vanilla extract

red wine vinegar
soy sauce
toasted sesame oil
tomato paste
tomato sauce
vegetable oil
white vinegar
Worcestershire sauce

ASSORTED DRIED SPICES

(to be replaced at least once a year)
basil
bay leaves
cayenne pepper
celery seed
chili powder
cinnamon
cloves
coriander
cumin
curry powder
dry mustard
garlic powder
ground ginger
mustard seed
nutmeg
onion powder
oregano
paprika
red pepper flakes
rosemary
sage
tarragon
thyme
whole black peppercorns

More Annoying Kitchen Tips® from Claud Mann, the TBS Food Guy

Take 5 minutes to read any recipe through before starting. Do you have the time, equipment and ingredients necessary?

• Attempt, whenever possible to use seasonal produce. This may even mean choosing a different recipe, but fruits and vegetables ALWAYS taste better and are cheaper in season. (How often do you get that combination?) This, by the way, is why so many great cooks appear so shifty when asked to give a recipe for a popular dish. Although some of them are undoubtedly truly shifty, the remainder know that duplication of their creation is virtually impossible without quality ingredients.

• The "resting" of meats after roasting isn't just a snooty term that gastronomes employ to sound superior (don't worry, they have plenty of others to fall back on). It's true, allowing a roast to sit at room temperature for even 5 or 10 minutes after leaving the oven allows any free-flowing juices an opportunity to retreat into the meat. Bottom line . . .you get a reputation for moist meat.

• The best cooks we know will taste a dish constantly as it cooks (not recommended, of course for pies and cakes) and before they actually begin cooking. If the apples are exceptionally sour or sweet, they know to adjust the sugar accordingly. One moment, a stew may taste just the way you want it, only to have the flavors flatten out the next. Tasting is the measure of a great cook.

• Don't be afraid to salt—at the right time. Proper salting can coax out a variety of flavors. Plus a pinch of salt in the kitchen can avoid a blizzard of salt at the table. One word of caution: never salt a dish you intend to reduce. As the liquid evaporates, it will become saltier than the tears you will shed when your guests take one taste and head off to the nearest restaurant.

• Clean as you work. (I don't, but my wife keeps saying it's a good habit to get into.)

• Calibrate your oven (and start your engines!). Actually, calibration is simply placing an accurate oven thermometer in the center of the oven and setting it to 350°F. If after 30 minutes, the thermometer reads more than 25 degrees off in either direction, call the gas company.

• Buy whole spices and grind them yourself. The easiest way is to keep an old coffee grinder around and grind just what you need. The taste difference is amazing.

• 15 minutes before serving, place plates in a 250°F. oven. It's very little trouble, shows your guests you care, and really does help keep food hot at the table.

Index

Appetizers, Dips:

Ballpark Pretzels, "Rolling in Dough" Homemade, 32

Bridget Fondue, 118

Heavenly Wings, 48

Mozzarella Marinara, Tony Manero's, 130

Offspring Rolls, 16

Parmesan Twists, 152

Sausage Nachos, Missing Link, 64

Secret Spy Snacks, 152

Steamin' Pork Buns, Jennifer's 70

Tacos, Bite Your Tongue, 94

Tempura, Extraterrestrial, 106

Turnovers, Mouthwatering Kathleen, 156

Two Hot Peppers on the Lamb, 142

Apples:

Carrie's Prom Crisp, 36

Christina Applecake, 56

Mouthwatering Kathleen Turnovers, 156

Scrooge's Crispy Gruel Stuffing, 38

Bacon:

Breakfast Club Sandwich, 30

Kevin Bacon and Cheese Hush Puppies, 74

Beans:

Bluto's Beer Chili, 108

Butcher Holler Ham Hocks and Collards, 42

Missing Link Sausage Nachos, 64

Patrick Swayze's Black-eyed Peas, 128

Sean Penne Pasta Salad, 68

Beef:

Baby Steppin' Kabobs, 158

Be All That You Can Beef Stroganoff, 140

Bite Your Tongue Tacos, 94

Bluto's Beer Chili, 108

Bumpin' Grinders, 54

Extra Cheesy Spielburgers, 122

Fall Apart Pot Roast, 98

I Want Liver Forever, I Wanna Learn How to Fry! 66

Road Trip Tri-Tip, 110

Soup on a Stick, 62

Standing Rib Roast with Rockshire Pudding, 72

Beer:

Bluto's Beer Chili, 108

Breads:

Biscuits to Die For (with One Foot in the Gravy), 46

Croutons, Young at Hearts of Romaine Salad, 80

Hush Puppies, Kevin Bacon and Cheese, 74

Soda Bread, Irish Stew for One, 114

Parmesan Twists, 152

"Pretzels, Rolling in Dough" Homemade Ballpark, 32

Breakfasts:

Peter Pancakes with Lost Boysenberry Syrup, 86

Buttermilk:

Biscuits to Die For (with One Foot in the Gravy), 46

Blues Brothers Funky Chicken, 28

Kevin Bacon and Cheese Hush Puppies, 74

Peter Pancakes with Lost Boysenberry Syrup, 86

Cabbage:

Male Chauvinist Pig, 10

Road Trip Tri-Tip, 110

Thai Noodles with Airplane Nuts, 12

Cheese:

Breakfast Club Sandwich, 30

Bridget Fondue, 118

Classic Cul-de-Sac Mac 'N Cheese, 34

Kevin Bacon and Cheese Hush Puppies, 74

Real Men's Quiche, 124

Tony Manero's Mozzarella Marinara, 130

Chicken:

Bigfoot Longs, 82

Blues Brothers Funky Chicken, 28

Extra Cheesy Spielburgers, 122

Soup on a Stick, 62

Thai Noodles with Airplane Nuts, 12

Triple Axel Rotisserie Chicken, 44

Index

Chocolate:
Bon Bons … James Bon Bons, 52
Golden Ladyfingers, 78

Desserts:
Bon Bons … James Bon Bons, 52
Breaker … Breaker Banana
  Cream Pie, 134
Carrie's Prom Crisp, 36
"Cherry Valence" Pie, 116
Christina Applecake, 56
Edible Fruitcake … No, Really!,
  40
Girls Just Wanna Have Flan, 104
Golden Ladyfingers, 78
Pecan Somebody Your Own Size
  Pie, 132
This Side-Upside-Down Cake,
  100

Drinks:
Ice Age Slushies, 64
Ice-Cold War Martinis, 152

Eggplant:
High Caliber Shells, 26

Eggs:
Girls Just Wanna Have Flan, 104
Real Men's Quiche, 124

**Entrees—Beef, Pork &
Lamb:**
Baby Steppin' Kabobs, 158
Be All That You Can Beef
  Stroganoff, 140
Bluto's Beer Chili, 108
Bumpin' Grinders, 54

Butcher Holler Ham Hocks and
  Collards, 42
Fall Apart Pot Roast, 98
I Want Liver Forever, I Wanna
  Learn How to Fry!, 66
Irish Stew for One, 114
Just the Facts, Ham, 60
Male Chauvinist Pig, 10
Patrick Swayze's Cracked Ribs
  and Black-eyed Peas, 128
Shrunken Shanks with Pygmy
  Veggies, 84
Soup on a Stick, 62
Standing Rib Roast with
  Rockshire Pudding, 72

Entrees—Poultry:
Big Jerked Chicken, 90
Blues Brothers Funky Chicken,
  28
"No Bull" Tequila Fajitas, 150
Scrooge's Turkey Legs with
  Crispy Gruel Stuffing, 38
Soup on a Stick, 62
Thai Noodles with Airplane Nuts,
  12
Triple Axel Rotisserie Chicken, 44

**Entrees—Fish &
Seafood:**
Creepy Crawly Crab Legs, 14
Dearly Departed Sole, 20
Extraterrestrial Tempura, 106
Man Eating Shark … and Loving
  It, 88
Miraculously Cured Salmon, 96
Mussels and Shrimp, 148
Napoleon "Bone-Apart" Snapper
  Sandwiches, 22

New Age Baloney, 92
"No Bull" Tequila Fajitas, 150
Nosferatuna Melts, 58
Sean Penne Pasta Salad, 68
Soup on a Stick, 62
Tommy's Tighty Whitey
  Whitefish, 126
Young-and-Naked Fish Kabobs
  with Mango Tiki Sauce, 24

Entrees—Vegetarian:
Bridget Fondue, 118
Classic Cul-de-Sac Mac 'N
  Cheese, 34
High Caliber Shells, 26
Offspring Rolls, 16
Super Extra Meaty Meat Loaf, 50
Travelin' Through Thyme and
  Onion Tart, 18

Fish:
Dearly Departed Sole, 20
Man Eating Shark … and Loving
  It, 88
Miraculously Cured Salmon, 96
Napoleon "Bone-Apart" Snapper
  Sandwiches, 22
New Age Baloney, 92
Nosferatuna Melts, 58
Sean Penne Pasta Salad, 68
Soup on a Stick, 62
Tommy's Tighty Whitey
  Whitefish, 126
Young-and-Naked Fish Kabobs
  with Mango Tiki Sauce, 24

Fruit:
Breaker … Breaker Banana
  Cream Pie, 134

Index

Carrie's Prom Crisp, 36

"Cherry Valence" Pie, 116

Christina Applecake, 56

Edible Fruitcake, 40

Ice Age Slushies, 64

Lost Boysenberry Syrup, 86

This Side-Upside-Down Cake, 100

Garlic:

Nosferatuna Melts, 58

Triple Axel Rotisserie Chicken, 44

Lamb:

Baby Steppin' Kabobs, 158

Extra Cheesy Spielburgers, 122

Irish Stew for One, 114

Shrunken Shanks with Pygmy Veggies, 84

Two Hot Peppers on the Lamb, 142

Nuts:

Bon Bons ... James Bon Bons, 52

Edible Fruitcake, 40

Offspring Rolls, 16

Pecan Somebody Your Own Size Pie, 132

Super Extra Meaty Meat Loaf, 50

Thai Noodles with Airplane Nuts, 12

Olives:

Bumpin' Grinders, 54

Julia's Angel Hair Puttanesca, 120

Travelin' Through Thyme and Onion Tart, 18

Triple Axel Rotisserie Chicken, 44

Onions:

Thyme and Onion Tart, Travelin' Through, 18

Pasta:

High Caliber Shells, 26

Julia's Angel Hair Puttanesca, 120

Sean Penne Pasta Salad, 68

Thai Noodles with Airplane Nuts, 12

Pie:

Breaker ... Breaker Banana Cream Pie, 134

"Cherry Valence" Pie, 116

Pecan Somebody Your Own Size Pie, 132

Pork:

Baby Steppin' Kabobs, 158

Jennifer's Steaming Pork Buns, 70

Just the Facts, Ham, 60

Male Chauvinist Pig, 10

Patrick Swayze's Cracked Ribs and Black-eyed Peas, 128

Salads:

Bean Salad, Sergeant Foley's Drop and Give Me 20, 112

New Age Baloney, 92

Pasta Salad, Sean Penne, 68

Rainforest Salad, Rapidly Disappearing, 96

Slaw, Road Trip Tri-Tip, 110

Young at Hearts of Romaine Seizure Salad, 80

Sandwiches:

Breakfast Club Sandwich, 30

Bumpin' Grinders, 54

Extra Cheesy Spielburgers, 122

Hollywood (Hulk) Hoagies, 102

Napoleon "Bone-Apart" Snapper Sandwiches, 22

Nosferatuna Melts, 58

Road Trip Tri-Tip, 110

Sauces:

Barbecue Sauce, Patrick Swayze's Moppin', 128

Barbecue Sauce, Road Trip Tri-Tip, 110

Curry Sauce, Creepy Crawly, 14

Horseradish Sauce, Standing Rib Roast, 72

Mango Tiki Sauce, Young-and-Naked Fish Kabobs, 24

Salsa, Bite Your Tongue 94

Salsa, "No Bull" Tequila Fajita, 150

Tartar Sauce, Napoleon "Bone-Apart" Snapper, 22

Tempura Dipping Sauce, Extra-terrestrial, 106

Tomatillo Sauce, Two Hot Peppers, 40

Zack Mayo, 112

Sausage:

Biscuits to Die For (with One Foot in the Gravy), 46

Bluto's Beer Chili, 108

Missing Link Sausage Nachos, 64

Real Men's Quiche, 124

Index

Scrooge's Turkey Legs with
  Crispy Gruel Stuffing, 38

Shrimp:

Extraterrestrial Tempura, 106

Mussels and Shrimp, 148

"No Bull" Tequila Fajitas, 150

Side Dishes:

Ballpark Pretzels, "Rolling in
  Dough" Homemade, 32

Gruel Stuffing, Scrooge's Crispy,
  38

Heavenly Wings, 48

Pork Buns, Jennifer's Steaming,
  70

Risotto, Italian Scallion, 138

Sausage Nachos, Missing Link,
  64

Soups:

Beer Chili, Bluto's, 108

Celery (Root of All Evil) Soup
  with Pork Belly (Bacon) Croutons,
  146

May the Borscht Be with You,
  136

Soup on a Stick, 62

Won Ton Soup, The Chosen 68

Turkey:

Scrooge's Turkey Legs with
  Crispy Gruel Stuffing, 38

Vegetables:

Collards, Butcher Holler Ham
  Hocks and, 42

Fries, "Pony Boy," 116

May the Borscht Be with You,
  136

Road Trip Slaw, 110

Vegetable Stock for Italian
  Scallion Risotto, 138

Credits & Acknowledgments

Project Manager and Editor—Tareion Fluker

Designer—Carley Wilson Brown

Creative Director—Pat Smith

Creative Coordinator—Kim Hyatt

Copy Editor—Gianna Messina

Assistant Copy Editors—Jennifer Ramseur, Ayanna Bennett,
Ben Applebaum and Michelle Waters

Additional Text—Jennifer Ramseur, Kathleen McTee, Robert Taylor and Gianna Messina

Illustrations—Robert Clyde Anderson

"Dinner & a Movie" Executive Producer—Kimberlee Carlson

Show Writers—Paul Gilmartin, Annabelle Gurwitch,
Rick Batalla, Tom Dorfmeister, Ashley Evans and Keith Merryman

Special Thanks to Clara Dowling, Bill Burke, Constance Barkley-Lewis,
Tobie H. Pate, Bill Cox, Jeff Carr, Tiffany Odom, Ward McCarthy, Jack Pendarvis,
Claudia Gomez, Richard Turner, Brent Sweitzer, Christine Corboy, Denise Bradshaw,
Daniel Hawley, Jennifer Stace, Larry Nicola, Gina McKenzie, Perla Batalla,
Heather McKenzie and Stephen Bedikian

P.O. Box 512 • Atlanta, Georgia 30301
TBSsuperstation.com